Historical Association Studies

Radicalism in the English
Revolution 1640–1660

Radicalism in the English Revolution 1640–1660

F. D. DOW

Basil Blackwell

© F.D. Dow 1985

First published 1985

Basil Blackwell Ltd
108 Cowley Road, Oxford OX4 1JF, UK

Basil Blackwell Inc.
432 Park Avenue South, Suite 1505,
New York, NY 10016, USA

British Library Cataloguing in Publication Data

Dow, F. D.
  Radicalism in the English Revolution: 1640–1660.
  —(Historical Association studies)
  1. Great Britain—History—Puritan Revolution, 1642–1660
  I. Title   II. Series
  942.06′3   DA405

  ISBN 0–631–13943–5

Library of Congress Cataloging in Publication Data

Dow, F. D.
  Radicalism in the English Revolution, 1640–1660.
  (Historical Association studies)
  Bibliography: p.
  Includes index.
  1. Great Britain—Politics and government—1642–1660.
  2. Radicalism—England—History—17th century.
  3. Levellers.   I. Title.   II. Series.
  DA405.D68   1985   941.6   84–29013

  ISBN 0–631–13943–5 (pbk.)

Typeset by Cambrian Typesetters, Frimley, Surrey
Printed in Great Britain by Whitstable Litho Ltd, Whitstable, Kent

Contents

Preface

This short study explores the nature and significance of radicalism in mid-seventeenth-century England in the light of recent historical research on the period of the Civil War. It does not attempt to provide a narrative history of these years but focuses instead on radical political and religious ideologies and their relationship to political action. The book emphasizes the ideological and organizational advances made by the Levellers, the Diggers and the sects, but it also examines the ideological continuities and bonds between the early 'conservative' opponents of the Stuart monarchy and those republican radicals of the later 1640s and 1650s who sought to reshape the established order in church and state. Successive chapters examine the nature of the beliefs which underpinned the challenge to established authority from within the ranks of the parliamentary cause in the early 1640s; the development of new and the refurbishment of old theories of political obligation in order to legitimize the English Republic; the significance of the Leveller movement and the nature of its programme; the ideological advances of the religious radicals and the sects; and the contribution to the history of radicalism made by the Diggers and the Clubmen. The reference list gives guidance for further reading.

F. D. Dow
University of Edinburgh

1 The Debate on the English Revolution

More than three hundred years after Charles I and Oliver Cromwell have left the stage, historians continue to debate the meaning and significance of the drama of the English Revolution. There has been an immense volume of research on the political, social and religious conflicts of mid-seventeenth-century England, but there is no overall agreement on the origins of the Civil War, the aims and methods of the protagonists in the struggle or the achievements of the victors. In particular, the role of radicalism is still in doubt. Were those who sought to transform the political and social order in Civil War England at best an insignificant minority, at worst a lunatic fringe, or were their ideals and aspirations central to the character of the parliamentary and republican regimes?

For at least a decade the thrust of much new research has been to impose a conservative interpretation on events. Most historians writing today have abandoned the search for long-term economic and social causes of the war and have concentrated on the short-term political ones. These political factors have frequently been explained in terms of personality and problems of 'management' rather than as the result of divisive issues or conflicting ideologies. Since the appearance of many local studies in the 1960s and 1970s, historians have stressed the cohesion of the county community on the eve of civil war, the strength of vertical social loyalties and the hold which ties of patronage and deference had on men. They are less likely to emphasize the disruptive effects of economic unrest and social disharmony or to believe that a class struggle was imminent. In place of the notion that during the 1640s large sections of those outside the elite may have responded with enthusiasm and commitment to the severing of the bonds of the old order, students are now assured that there was widespread popular neutralism and disinclination to become involved in a nationwide, ideological struggle. Even such a seemingly revolutionary body as the New Model Army has been presented to us recently in a profoundly conservative guise. And as

1

for the outcome of the struggle, it is now difficult to cast either the intentions or the effect of republican rule in anything more sweeping than a moderate, reformist light. The Rump Parliament (1649–53), we are told, was predominantly moderate, even conservative, in its objectives, and neither the Commonwealth nor the Protectorate saw a breach in the traditional ruling classes' stranglehold of power in the localities.

Against these claims, however, some writers have continued to assert that even though radicalism did not conquer the citadels of power in mid-seventeenth-century England, popular pressure and radical agitation deeply affected the political and intellectual climate of these years. The most eloquent expression of this view, and the most compelling affirmation of the belief that radicalism mattered in the English Revolution, has come from the pen of Christopher Hill. In a series of books dealing with the Levellers, the Diggers, the religious radicals, Gerrard Winstanley and John Milton among others, Hill has highlighted the flowering of radical, democratic and egalitarian notions among the common people. Although frequently criticized for exaggerating the influence and appeal of these ideals, Hill's picture of a radical plebeian culture cannot be ignored. The significance of his work and that of other likeminded historians prompts the question: can radicalism be put into a new perspective which takes into account the convincing arguments of the conservative 'revisionists' but yet leaves room for the belief that there really was a 'revolution' in England in the 1640s and 1650s? The following chapters will attempt a reassessment of the radicals in this light, but first it will be helpful to examine in more detail some recent contributions to the wider debate on the English Revolution.

Numerous historians have concerned themselves with the origins of the Civil War. Their work has therefore not provided direct answers to many of the most pressing questions about the importance of radical ideas and activity *after* the outbreak of fighting, but their findings have undoubtedly predisposed other writers to look at the aims of the parliamentarians and their supporters in a sceptical, conservative light. There have been roughly three related approaches to the origins of the conflict: historians have examined the nature of parliamentary politics before 1640; they have explored the relationship between the centre and the localities in this period; and they have examined the aims and objectives of Charles I and the Court during the Personal Rule.

Conrad Russell has been the most influential among the historians of parliament (1976, 1979, 1983). He has argued forcefully against the old 'Whig-liberal' notion that from at least the 1620s, if not before, there existed an opposition in the House of Commons whose fight to protect the liberties of the subject against the encroachments of royal prerogative forced it into inevitable conflict with the Crown. On the contrary, Russell and his disciples have contended, there was no such thing as an 'opposition' in early Stuart parliaments, and certainly not one which reflected the gentry's permanent desire to obstruct the policies of the Crown. Parliamentary struggles (in which the House of Lords was likely to play a more important part than the Commons) were usually the result of a spillover of faction fights at Court. Contentious debates were more likely to be instigated by discontented peers or members of the Privy Council than by a 'Country' opposition in the lower house, and the pressures of local politics were more important to MPs than the furthering of grandiose constitutional ambitions. There was no steady increase in tension between 1604 and 1642 and links between disputes in the 1620s and those in the Long Parliament between 1640 and 1642 were tenuous in the extreme. There is thus no question of an 'inevitable' breakdown in relations between the two opposing sides, 'Crown' and 'parliament' (Rabb, 1981). The implication of this view is that the political crisis of 1640–2 could not have been caused by the existence of a party among the gentry with radical political ambitions.

Complementing this analysis of politics at Westminster is the large volume of work, much of it assessed and commented upon by John Morrill in his influential introduction to *The Revolt of the Provinces* (1976), which stresses the significance of the local dimension to politics. The 'county community' school of thought was originally inspired by Alan Everitt's *The Community of Kent and the Great Rebellion* (1966) and has been elaborated in a succession of admirable local studies, including Morrill on Cheshire (1974), Fletcher on Sussex (1975) and Underdown on Somerset (1973). Designed originally as a response to the search for the possible social origins of the Civil War and in particular to the 'storm over the gentry', the 'county community' school has profoundly influenced our view of political relationships on the eve of the crisis. Like the work on parliament, local studies have underlined the essential moderation and conservatism of Charles's future parliamentary opponents and they have tended to minimize the possibility of deep-seated social antagonism in the counties from which popular radical demands might spring.

Several aspects of these local studies are particularly important. First, they are based on the premiss that 'each county had its own status hierarchy and its own political culture' (Underdown, 1980) and that each county's experience before and during the war was unique and deserves to be studied in its own right. The search for national political trends is therefore misplaced. The gentry's primary loyalty was to their immediate community and they were interested principally in local issues, not national ones. Such worries as they had about the actions of the Crown in the 1630s were the result of the *effects* of royal policies as experienced in a strictly local context. They were not concerned about the wider constitutional implications of royal measures on a national scale, and the strength of the gentry's local concerns, not their views on such general questions as 'the constitution' or the 'liberties of the subject', was therefore paramount in forming their attitudes to the political crisis of 1640.

On the other hand, we are warned that this predominantly localist frame of reference should not be taken to mean that the gentry were opposed to or wished to be isolated from the Crown. On the contrary, they were only too aware of their links with the Crown through the operation of the patronage network and their predisposition to obey royal authority – the 'momentum of obedience' on which Charles could rely – was strong and long-lasting. It was only when the outbreak of the Bishops' Wars with the Scots placed extra financial and administrative burdens on the shires that many gentry began to feel that the maintenance of their local interests might compel them to take remedial action against the Crown. Consequently opposition to Crown policy which was expressed in 1640 was not the result of long-held constitutional ambitions or a deep-seated lust for national power on the part of the gentry but, more prosaically, the result of short-term exasperation and impatience with the effects of royal policy in the localities.

Not inconsistent with this explanation of the crisis of 1640 is the viewpoint which stresses that Charles I's period of personal rule was an innovative one, in which the King and his advisers went on to the offensive in many aspects of royal policy towards church, state and society (Sharpe, 1983). In matters of religion especially, Charles's support for Laud and Arminianism marked a break with the past which upset the deeply traditionalist gentry (Tyacke, 1973), but the tendency was also to be found in financial and administrative developments (D. Thomas, 1983). This line of argument connects with other elements in the conservative case to bolster the view that the men who came to Westminster in 1640 were as opposed to change as they were to Charles I, and that the very last thing most of them wanted was to subvert the existing constitution or alter the traditional order of things in the name of 'progress' or 'revolution'. In 1640 very few of them even contemplated a resort to arms. At Westminster debates in the Long Parliament continued to be couched in traditionalist terms which emphasized the links between royal and parliamentary interests and the need to restore the balance of the old constitution. In the localities, the extreme reluctance of the gentry to take sides was reflected in petitions to both Crown and parliament to compose their differences and in frantic attempts in many counties and boroughs to form neutrality pacts to prevent the outbreak of fighting.

These arguments about the aspirations of the gentry and the nature of the county community have convinced many historians, but they leave out of account some important pressures and influences which were working on the governing classes and which on closer examination give a different dimension to the conflict. Brian Manning, for example, has forcefully argued that economic discontent and popular unrest were important elements in producing an atmosphere of crisis before and after 1640 (1976). Pointing to the large number of popular disturbances in the counties, especially enclosure riots and other demonstrations of hostility towards the rich, and to the existence of much popular agitation in London between 1640 and 1642, he has argued that this eruption of the lower and middling orders into the political arena crucially affected the alignment of political groupings within the elite. In his view what principally distinguished royalists from parliamentarians by 1642 was not their attitude to constitutional reform or political change but their attitude to 'the people'. More fitting labels for Charles I and his opponents, Manning says, would really be 'the party of order' and 'the popular party', for there is a stark and fundamental contrast between the willingness of the parliamentarians to harness 'the people' to their cause and the desire of the royalists to repress them. Parliament's appeal to 'the middle sort of people' was in turn to release one of the most dynamic forces of the decade and substantially promote the cause of popular radicalism.

Few writers would go as far as Manning in ascribing to the 'governed' a truly formative role in the crisis, but he is not alone in pointing to the existence of social unrest and political interest outside the ranks of the elite. Much recent work on riot and popular disturbance confirms that the poor could organize themselves in defence of economic rights and privileges and take effective direct action (B. Sharp, 1980; Walter, 1980; Walter and Wrightson, 1976; Lindley, 1982). Other studies suggest that the expansion of the electorate in the early seventeenth century enabled the substantial middling orders to become involved in the political disputes of their superiors (Hirst, 1975) and that the gentry were aware of the need to placate their opinion at least in the crucial matter of taxation (Hill, 1981). Recent work by Anthony Fletcher (1981) shows that between 1640 and 1642 informed political opinion in the localities was not confined to the ruling elite. The middling orders were involved in political debate and participated in petitioning campaigns, but Fletcher emphasizes that they did not hold the political initiative.

5

Overall, then, the conservative case is secure when it maintains that radical demands and popular agitation were not the causes of the Civil War, but enough evidence remains to suggest that radicalism might have been the outcome of the struggle.

Conservative historians would, however, resist the notion that when the elite took up arms against each other, this was in itself sufficient to arouse dormant radical forces. Quite rightly they have focused on several areas where it is dangerous to exaggerate the break with the past. They have stressed that in the early months of the fighting both sides found it extremely difficult to build up military support in the face of widespread neutralism, and that throughout the war years the battle to win the hearts and minds of the local communities was at least as difficult as the struggle against the opposing army. This is a recurrent theme in many of the contributions to a recent statement of the conservative case, John Morrill (ed.), *Reactions to the English Civil War 1642–1649* (1982). But, as Morrill has constantly reminded us, neutralism was not the same as apathy: there was such a thing as active neutralism, a determination to protect local political interests and to preserve existing social and economic patterns which when threatened could take on a militant guise. Such a desire had influenced the attempted neutrality pacts of the local gentry in 1642. It later informed a more popular kind of localist resistance, the Clubmen Associations in the south and west of England in 1645 and 1646. Formed to resist the depredations of war no matter by whom they were perpetrated, these essentially peasant movements were profoundly conservative in their aims (the preservation of property and the restoration of the old order in church and state were favourite themes), although arguably they were extremely radical in their methods. Ideologically akin to the provincial conservatism of the pre-war gentry, these examples of popular political activity have played a crucial part in the conservative argument that there was no innate or necessary connection between radicalism and the people in the 1640s. The Clubmen's defence of the traditional order was, asserts Morrill with some force, more characteristic of the later 1640s than the iconoclasm of the Levellers (1976). Once again, an important social group is depicted as resistant to, not desirous of, change.

The New Model Army has recently received similar treatment. Mark Kishlansky has subjected the composition and aims of this body to close scrutiny (1979b). He maintains that the army was not a radical force from the outset and that its composition and the promotions policy which operated within it were entirely conventional. It became politicized only in 1647 in response to parliament's refusal to remedy its material grievances, especially its arrears of pay. Its motive was to vindicate its own conduct and maintain its own honour, and its desire to protect past liberties, both for itself and for the citizenry, was more important than the wish to demand new rights. The influence of sectarians within the army and the pressure from London-based radicals had less effect on the army's revolutionary impetus than the soldiers' spontaneous reaction to the demands of the Presbyterian faction in the House of Commons. Although for a time in the autumn of 1647 the soldiers' grievances blended with those of the Levellers, the two movements were essentially separate and divergent. Mistrust of both King and parliament, not commitment to the radical cause, was the driving force behind the army. Only when the impossibility of reaching an agreement with Charles was brought home to the leaders of the army after the second civil war did they reluctantly decide to purge parliament and execute the King. Thus Charles by his own actions in 1648 had done more to seal his fate than had all the efforts of John Lilburne.

Current research on political opinion at Westminster likewise discourages the hasty assumption that radical sentiment was gaining ground. From the start there had been some hardliners who undoubtedly wished to press on to outright victory against the King, but even when parliament split into more polarized political groupings in the mid–1640s there were few even among the Independents who contemplated an eventual settlement which would break decisively with the past. Within the House of Commons, men such as Edmund Ludlow, Arthur Hesilrige and Henry Marten constituted a radical core who could look for support to 'honest radicals' in the counties and in London, but until trust in Charles had been finally destroyed in 1648 very few men thought about the abolition of monarchy. The path to regicide was therefore marked out by exasperation with a perfidious King and by a realization that the burdens of renewed war would provoke a conservative reaction among the people, rather than by the hope of transforming the political and social order. Indeed very few even of the regicides were revolutionaries at heart. Only about seventy members of the Rump Parliament associated themselves with the proceedings between Pride's Purge on 6 December 1648 and the King's execution on 30 January 1649, and only forty-three of these signed Charles's death warrant. Many of the Rumpers and some of the regicides went as far as they did only because of a desire to preserve the gains already made and to stem further progress towards revolution, not to encourage it. Only by accepting the King's execution could they, they believed, stop a complete take-over by the army or prevent a sell-out to Levellers or wild sectaries. As more members began to trickle back to the House in February and

7

March 1649, this moderate, even conservative, temper in the Commons was reinforced. The execution of the King may therefore have been a revolutionary act, but not all of those who approved of it or condoned it were revolutionaries (Worden, 1974).

These arguments in support of the 'revisionist' case are powerful, but they neglect alternative considerations more conducive to the 'radical' case. Many of these points will be elaborated in the following chapters. In the first place, it has to be recognized that as the war progressed some parliamentarians were driven to justify their resistance to their anointed King with novel arguments that questioned traditional assumptions about the political order (see chapter 2). The methods which parliament employed to sustain its war effort also led to some startling changes in the structure of local government. Established institutions were radically altered to raise men and money for the cause, while the traditional rulers of the counties were often pushed aside by men of stronger ideological commitment but of lesser social rank. Nor can it be disputed that among the parliamentary armies the Puritan 'middle sort' were to play an important role. These developments interacted with other longstanding economic and social grievances to prompt a minority within the lower and middling orders to seek new political and religious solutions to their problems. In so doing they created an atmosphere of intellectual excitement and stimulation quite un-rivalled in the period before the French Revolution. Ideological and organizational advances were made by radicals which were not matched until the 1760s. Although the Levellers did not achieve power, and succeeded more in frightening those who did hold power than in convincing them of the merits of the radical case, their beliefs and their programme opened up new vistas of political participation, religious toleration and social equality if not for all men then at least for very significant sections of the middling classes (see chapter 3). Likewise, the leading exponents of religious radicalism provided a dazzling array of innovative notions about God, sin, heaven, hell and all creation. The shock which greeted their wilder excesses should not obscure their seminal contribution to the debate on the relations between church, state and society (see chapter 4).

The toleration which many religious radicals enjoyed under the English Republic is in itself a powerful argument against the view that the conservative case also applies to the governments of the Interregnum. Here again, a close analysis of the Rump Parliament has produced the opinion that this body was composed essentially of moderates, was uninterested in ideology, and concentrated instead, despite a few bursts of reforming enthusiasm, on making day-to-day government work (Worden, 1974). The authors of local studies have also confirmed that in the counties many attempted reforms in the early days of the Republic and again in 1655–6, foundered against the strength of existing structures and institutions. The cohesion of local society was ultimately proof against the reforming zeal of a handful of parliamentary radicals and a clutch of Major-Generals. The survival of Anglican ceremonies in many parish churches is also adduced to show the strength of popular traditionalism (Morrill, 1982). The Protectorate is viewed either as a step on the inevitable path to the restoration of monarchy or, at best, as a conservative reaction to the insecurity and instability of the Commonwealth. The radicals are therefore relegated to the role of ineffectual pressure groups whose ideas and aspirations were not integral to the character of the Republic. Their very limited influence is seen as negative rather than positive, a destabilizing force which threatened even the moderate gains of the Revolution.

Yet, as the following chapters show, this is not the whole story. The need to legitimize the Republic brought to the fore radical new theories of political obligation. Moreover, the moderates in the Commonwealth and the Protectorate parliaments were never quite able to conquer those true republican enthusiasts for the 'Good Old Cause' whose arguments in favour of a new type of balanced constitution held open the prospect of a more liberal political order (see chapter 2). It would also be wrong to draw too stark an antithesis between the 'conservatism' of the men who actually governed English in the 1650s and the 'radicalism' of their critics, for, as Austin Woolrych has recently reminded us, a tension between radical Puritanism and gentry constitutionalism was inherent in all the regimes of the English Republic (1982). Thus the periodic attempts to reform the law and the clergy cannot be ignored, and the policy of toleration, with its attempts to balance a variety of competing social, economic and religious interests, needs to be borne in mind. Above all, the ability of religious radicalism to flourish in this allegedly conservative climate deserves close study (see chapter 4).

Radicalism therefore has been pushed out of the limelight by the work of conservative historians. From the viewpoint of a historian of political events there is undoubtedly much justice in this. The immediate political influence and effectiveness of the radicals has in the past been overstressed. But no historian of political ideas can afford to deny the radicals a leading part. Their contributions to the debate on popular rights and liberties was immense. Moreover, their very existence was an essential element in forming the climate of opinion in mid-seventeenth-century England. Whether by a process of attraction or repulsion it was they who convinced contemporaries that the world was not the same way up as it had been in 1640.

2 Parliamentarians and Republicans

'Revisionist' historians have accustomed us to the idea that before and after 1640 the aims and actions of the political elite were marked by caution, conservatism and a resistance to change. Similarly the ideas and arguments which the opponents of the Crown put forward to justify their position for a long time showed a disinclination to break free from traditional modes of political thought. Radical theories about the origins, nature and purpose of political power may have been the eventual by-product of the Civil War, but they were assuredly not its cause. On the contrary, the debates in the Long Parliament from 1640 to 1642 made it clear that Charles I and his critics shared many political assumptions and many social ideals. Only in the face of armed conflict did some parliamentary apologists branch out in new directions to justify resistance to their king, but even then they were extremely reluctant to draw radical or democratic conclusions from their arguments. Although various arguments about popular consent and the role of the common people in the struggle were put forward in the Civil War years, and so provided the material on which later political and religious radicalism could build, the parliamentarians in the 1640s were essentially concerned to justify the interests of the elite against the Crown, not to advocate a widespread extension of political and social power to those lower down the scale. Likewise when the army and the Rump were faced with the problem of proving the legitimacy of the new Republic, not all the arguments they employed necessarily pointed in a democratic or even a liberal direction. By the 1650s the contention that the origin of government lies in the consent of the people had gained wider acceptance among those in power, but republicans of many hues still hesitated to concede that *active* political rights should be widely dispersed and preferred instead to uphold a distinction between the 'few' and the 'many' in the actual working of government. None the less, great strides had been made in theorizing about government – an intellectual gain if not a practical political

10

one – with two of the most notable contributions coming from Thomas Hobbes and James Harrington, each of whom profoundly influenced the future course of political thought.

The Defence of the Old Order

Before the outbreak of civil war several ideas about the nature of the political and social order were widely, almost universally, accepted throughout the political nation. There was a strong belief in the 'divine right of kings', that is the notion that God had directly ordained kings to rule and that they were therefore his lieutenants on earth. Many writers likened the King's authority to that of a patriarch, and sustained this argument with examples from the Bible to show that God had intended human society to be ruled by patriarchs at every level. Thus the patriarchal authority of the divinely ordained King at the top of the political structure was reflected lower down the social and political scale in the analogous authority of all 'governors', be they justices of the peace, minor officials or even simply masters and employers. Religious sanctions were heavily invoked to uphold this argument: the injunction to 'honour thy father and thy mother' in the fifth commandment was interpreted to mean, in the words of one catechism, 'not only natural parents but all superiors in age and gifts, and especially such as by God's ordinance are over us in places of authority, whether in family, church or commonwealth' (A. Sharp, 1983, p. 27). The church too played an extremely significant part in propagating other notions on the duty of the subject to obey the 'powers that be', notions which were endorsed by all those in the ruling classes who had a vested interest in supporting a stable and hierarchical political and social order. Biblical texts such as that in Romans 13 were used repeatedly to impress upon the population the sinfulness as well as the futility of all disorder and rebellion: 'Let every soul be subject to the higher powers', the pulpits would thunder, 'For there is no power but of God: the powers that be are ordained of God. Whosoever therefore resisteth the power, resisteth the ordinance of God: and they that resist . . . shall receive to themselves damnation.'

Other aspects of contemporary social thought reinforced these political tenets by upholding the ideal of a static, harmonious universe. The social doctrine of the 'great chain of being' put forward the view that the law of nature and the command of God sustained a system of order and harmony based on rank, status and hierarchy throughout all creation. This divine and natural pattern comprehended everything and everybody from archangels to inanimate objects like trees and rocks. Human society was a microcosm of the

11

whole with a fixed place for everyone from the King at the top down to the humblest subject. Attempts to rebel against or change this order could only produce disaster and confusion.

These arguments in favour of order, authority and hierarchy were not seriously undermined or challenged in political debate in England before 1640. In retrospect it is possible to see that other ideas were being aired which did not sit easily beside this orthodoxy, but the threat was potential rather than actual. In various ways Puritan writers kept to the fore the notion that the claims of God and of conscience might take precedence over those of the King, but in the early seventeenth century they did not extend their ideas into a coherent theory of, or a practical plan for, resistance. Likewise Puritan ideas about godly reform and the regeneration of society were not entirely consistent with the notion of a naturally harmonious universe, but their implications lay politically dormant. What clergymen and preachers might write was not, at least on the Puritan side, the same thing as what laymen and politicans might do. In the short term the desire for social control and political order was paramount. Even so staunch an advocate of later resistance as John Lilburne accepted before 1640 that the doctrines of non-resistance and passive obedience should be observed.

The very large measure of agreement within the political nation on the structure of established authority did not preclude disagreement on how government might actually work, or on how royal power should be exercised in practice. Critics of the Crown before and after the meeting of the Long Parliament did not accuse Charles and his apologists of inventing a new type of government, far less claim to be doing so themselves; rather they complained that the King was not properly abiding by the rules of the old order. In particular they argued that although in theory the King possessed wide prerogative powers, in practice the manner in which he exercised them was contrary to the laws of the land and was threatening to upset the delicate balance between the powers of the Crown, the privileges of parliament and the liberties of the subject on which the constitution rested. In so doing they were not challenging royal authority as such, but they were saying that it should not be taken out of context. Their definition of that context relied heavily on notions of law. References to the laws of the land and to a fundamental law on which the constitution rested were crucial motifs in the arguments of the Crown's opponents from 1640 to 1642 and continued greatly to influence parliamentary theories of resistance after war broke out. Such arguments allowed the parliamentarians to appear in a traditionalist guise and, although they buttressed the authority of the parliamentary classes against the Crown, they did not easily lend themselves to use by those who wished to assert the right of the common people to an active say in affairs.

The standard parliamentary position on the origins and nature of the constitution was also based on notions of history and experience. Many of its key elements had been raised in debates in parliament in the 1620s and it owed much to the writings of Sir Edward Coke. From 1600 onwards Sir Edward (who before his death in 1634 had been Lord Chief Justice and a prominent MP) had attempted to synthesize and systematize the vast mass of English case law and statutes; in so doing he produced an interpretation of the law which was 'favourable to the rights of the subject and restrictive of the royal prerogative' (Woolrych, 1980, p. 41). But he also developed a powerful historical myth about the law and the nature of the constitution which the Long Parliament found extremely compelling. Coke claimed that the origins of the law lay in Anglo-Saxon times and that its principles had been maintained against the encroachments of Norman kingship by the vigilance of the English people and their representatives in parliament. Large sections of Coke's theory were incorporated into the Long Parliament's own arguments and they formally ordered the first complete publication of Coke's *Institutes* in 1641. By 1641 three notions, those of fundamental law, common law and the ancient constitution, had become confused and combined to produce in the minds of many parliamentarians a distinctive vision of a balanced polity whose equilibrium had been upset by the actions of the King, but which it was now parliament's task to correct and protect. The extremely vague and ill-defined concept of an unwritten 'fundamental law' or laws which set out the functions of all elements in the balanced polity including the royal prerogative, and which the King was now in danger of transgressing, was used in conjunction with the less abstract argument that the King's actions were also threatening the law of the land, that is the common law. To the common law some parliamentarians seemed prone to attribute mystical properties. Sir Edward Coke had argued that common law was customary and immemorial (that is, traceable to no act of foundation), that it was immutable in its basic principles, but yet embodied the wisdom of generations and the refinements of experience. It had been confirmed by time, by generations of English people *and* by generations of English monarchs. It was, indeed, the continuous voice of the monarch providing justice for his people, and so superior to the judgements of any one particular ruler. Coke had then extended his argument to the fundamental principles of the constitution, which was also immemorial and prescriptive (that is, sanctioned by experience). This ancient constitution was itself in some way ultimately immune from prerogative action, and although its principles were consistent with the King's possession of prerogative power they enshrined also the privileges of parliament and the liberties of the subject. Thus parliament too had an immemorial history (Pocock, 1957). By 1641 these notions were widely current in parliamentary circles. Fundamental law, common law and the ancient constitution all required that the King's recent actions be carefully scrutinized.

Many parliamentarians were, however, still very reluctant to accuse the King personally of upsetting the balance of the constitution. They preferred instead to find a scapegoat, an evil councillor, whom they could charge with subverting the course of royal policy. For a long time, indeed, critics of the Crown had been eager to attribute royal failings to the influence of 'Papists' at Court, and linked with this alleged papist conspiracy was Thomas Wentworth, Earl of Strafford. He was chosen as the chief scapegoat. The charges made against Strafford in 1640, and the speeches made at his trial in 1641, illustrate many of the themes we have noticed so far in parliamentarian thinking, while also showing how narrow was the gap in political argument between the Crown and its opponents. In making the preliminary charges against Strafford in November 1640, John Pym had assured his listeners that 'it is the law that unites the King and his people' and that the Commons were far from desiring 'any abridgement of those great prerogatives which belong to the King; they know that their own liberty and peace are preserved and secured by his prerogative'; none the less Strafford had attempted to come between King and people and upset the temper of the body politic. In April 1641 at Strafford's trial, Pym elaborated: 'The Law is the boundary, the measure between the King's prerogative and the people's liberty', but added, with an eye to the prospect of anarchy as well as tyranny, 'if you take away the law all things will fall into a confusion, every man will become a law to himself . . . the law hath a power to prevent, to restrain, to repair evils; without this all kinds of mischief and distempers will break in upon a State.' Ironically Strafford too had accepted that 'the happiness of a kingdom consists in [the] just poise of the King's prerogative and the subject's liberty', had rhetorically asked his peers 'do we not live by laws' and had accused Pym and his allies of subverting the laws of the kingdom (Kenyon, 1966, pp. 206–16).

Strafford's execution in May 1641 did cause some to wonder if the earl had not been right after all, and this and other hard-line tactics of Pym and his allies alienated some moderate opinion. Yet the Irish Rebellion in the following autumn (apparent proof of the alleged papist menace) and, later, Charles's evident untrustworthiness over such matters as the attempted arrest of the Five Members in January

1642 cemented the loyalty of others to the anti-Court position. As the political nation slid into war, many continued to argue that parliament was acting to preserve the ancient constitution and the laws of the land, but other more discerning thinkers on the parliamentary side realized that with the taking up of arms the arguments in favour of resistance had to be moved on to new ground.

The Justification of Resistance

Men who had spent a good part of their lives absorbing the implications of the fifth commandment and of Romans 13 did not, even with the common law behind them, find it easy to justify a civil war. The historian J.W. Allen commented that, to judge by their writings, many parliamentarian apologists might have anticipated Oscar Wilde's advice to young scribes: 'Never be intelligible', Wilde opined; 'To be intelligible is to be found out' (Allen, 1938, p. 469). Certainly there is a lack of coherence in the parliamentary case, and, right up to 1649, theoretical justification for its actions was never clear-cut, nor based on a single concept (Judson, 1949, p. 378). Some parliamentarians never got beyond the 'evil councillors' argument, believing always that they were fighting a papist conspiracy, while others simply took their stand on their right to resist the enforcement of illegal claims or unlawful commands. Other writers however advanced more positive claims for parliament, and produced arguments with greater potential for later political radicalism. At the time, these authors were concerned primarily with the struggle against the Crown, not with the possibility of using these arguments to sustain a new political order, but many of their ideas formed the essential precursors to later Leveller thought.

Four major issues were touched on by these 'new' writers: the nature and location of sovereignty; the origins of government in the consent of the people; the welfare of the people as the end or purpose of government; and the role of the common people in resisting the King. The arguments deployed were not wholly novel in the canons of political thought, but they took on new significance in the context of the practical politics of the time. They were employed not merely to justify resistance, but also in the first instance to counter the propaganda of the King, who established the framework for political debate on the outbreak of war by putting forward a rival view of the balanced constitution which his opponents could not ignore.

In his answer to the Nineteen Propositions presented to him by parliament in June 1642, Charles rested his case on a theory of mixed monarchy. This was not in itself original, for theories of mixed government (that is, that government should combine three kinds of rule: monarchical, aristocratic and democratic) had their antecedents in classical and Renaissance learning and had been aired in England in the sixteenth century. Moreover, the idea that the 'ancient constitution' was a mixed government was inherent in the historical myths propagated by Coke, for the fundamental principles of that constitution included a role for King, Lords and Commons. (As we shall see, overtly republican versions of 'mixed government' were to be current in the 1650s.) The notion of 'mixture' in government thus spanned the centuries, but in 1642 Charles's particular exposition of mixed *monarchy* was designed to show that it was parliament and not he who was threatening to upset the balance of the constitution. Charles accepted that there were three 'pure' forms of government – monarchy, aristocracy and democracy. Each in itself had obvious virtues or conveniences: monarchy could take swift action in times of emergency; aristocracy could provide the wise counsel of a 'few' for the public benefit; and democracy could foster the courage and industry of the free citizen. But each by itself could lead to vice or inconvenience: monarchy would degenerate into tyranny; aristocracy into faction and division; and democracy into anarchy and licentious-ness. Fortunately for England, Charles asserted:

> The experience and wisdom of your Ancestors hath so moulded this [government] out of a mixture of these [elements], as to give to this Kingdom . . . the conveniences of all three, without the inconveniences of any one, as long as the Balance hangs even between the three Estates [the King, the House of Lords and the House of Commons], and they run joyntly on in their proper Chanell . . . (quoted in Weston, 1960, p. 428)

Several parliamentarian writers responded to the challenge set down by Charles I's version of the theory of mixed monarchy. Three of the most significant were Philip Hunton, Charles Herle and, most important of all, Henry Parker. Each moved away from the use of arguments based on law to arguments based on the needs and rights of the people, and in so doing began to grapple with concepts of sovereignty and of popular consent.

In *A Treatise of Monarchie* (1643), Philip Hunton accepted that English government was a mixed monarchy in which the King was limited by law, but he also saw that there must be a real sovereign power in government. Hunton accepted the sixteenth-century French philosopher Jean Bodin's definition of sovereignty as 'the power to make law', and accordingly located this power in the King-in-parliament. He went on to deny that the King could possess any considerable power outside parliament, for the governing power of the King could not be independent of the legislative power, which was the supreme power. However, if King and parliament disagreed over their respective functions, neither had the right to set itself up as the final arbiter. To do so would upset the very balance which was the essence of the mixture. If either became arbiter, it would then become the sovereign power, and supremacy would no longer rest with the 'mixture' of King, Lords and Commons (Judson, 1949). As an attempt to provide a clear-cut justification for parliament's actions Hunton's acute constitutional analysis was a failure, although Hunton himself did urge people to support the parliamentary cause. His theories did, however, point to the fact that recourse to the law could not solve political problems, and that the political nation would have to confront the issue of where sovereignty lay. Moreover, in his analysis of sovereignty he was brought to concede that power was ultimately derived from the people, for he asserted that 'consent and fundamental contract of a nation was the root of all sovereignty'. In 1644 he affirmed that originally men possessed a 'virtuall radicall power by publike consent and contract to constitute this or that forme of Government' (quoted in Judson, 1949, p. 398).

More vigorous and politically effective than Hunton were Charles Herle and Henry Parker. Herle, like Hunton, saw English government as a mixed monarchy, but he more successfully dealt with the need to justify resistance by admitting that only political control by the people in parliament could secure redress against a monarch who broke the law. Henry Parker, a lawyer and son of a Sussex landowner, was one of the most impressive writers on the parliamentary side and deserves much more attention from historians of radicalism than he usually receives. His services to parliament won him some reward; in 1642 he was appointed secretary to the Earl of Essex's army and in 1645 he was made secretary to the Commons. He spelled out his views on government in a series of pamphlets between 1642 and 1644, of which the most famous are *Observations Upon Some of His Majesties Late Answers and Expresses* (1642), a direct riposte to Charles's answer to the Nineteen Propositions, and *Ius Populi* (1644).

The basis for his views was a belief in the consent of the people as the origin of government. 'Power is originally inherent in the people', he declared; and again 'power is but secondary and derivative in Princes, the foundation and efficient cause is the people' (Erskine-Hill and Storey, 1983, pp. 36–7). Thus Parker supported in peace time a limited monarchy with the powers of the Crown constrained, and occupying a subordinate place in the constitution. In 1644, in pursuit of a sound justification for parliamentary resistance, Parker also focused on the purpose of government: the welfare of the people was the end of government, he argued, for 'Princes were created by the people, for the peoples sake, and so limited by expresse Laws as that they might not violate the peoples liberty' (quoted in Judson, 1949, p. 417). If princes failed to act in the interests of the people, Parker concluded, then parliament (representing the whole people) had the right to act to restrain the monarch. In these circumstances parliament could assess the needs of the people without reference to the King and could take appropriate measures including legislative action without him. In the last analysis, therefore, parliament's power was both sovereign and arbitrary.

During the period of the Civil War, Parker's stress on popular consent as the origin of government was far from unique, but his willingness to grapple with the problem of sovereignty was distinctive. His ideas marked a significant break with the traditional legalistic arguments of the opposition in 1640–2, and to contemporaries they seemed daringly radical. However, it is important also to recognize their limitations. Despite their intellectual debt to Parker, it was the Levellers' sense of these limitations that propelled them on a more truly radical and democratic course later in the decade. First, Parker's theories did not in themselves provide a justification for republicanism; indeed not even the person of Charles I, still less the office of King, was attacked in the *Observations*. Second, parliament's right to act to correct the excesses of a monarch was explicitly deemed to be merely a reactive, defensive right; it could come into play to protect the welfare of the people only after the King had betrayed their trust and had 'deserted' the people; parliament for its part had no right to take the initiative and 'desert' the King. Third, and most important, Parker (together with Charles Herle and other theorists of popular consent) was adamant that the people could not exercise their power outside parliament. Despite being the originators of government, the people could exercise their right of resistance only in and through parliament. Parker refused to recognize that the interests and wishes of people and parliament might not coincide. In his view, parliament perfectly represented the people – indeed *was* the people, or as Charles Herle put it, 'The Parliament *is* the people's own consent, which once passed, they cannot revoke . . . We acknowledge no power can be employed but what is reserved and the people have reserved no power from themselves in Parliament' (A. Sharp, 1983, p. 73).

On this point the Levellers were to part company with moderates like Parker and Herle, for they could envisage only too clearly a distinction between the political interests of parliament and those of the people. As we shall see in chapter 3, the desire to 'reserve' certain powers to the people as a whole, and a disinclination to entrust the consideration of certain important matters to the legislature, was a prominent feature of the Leveller programme. Parker and his fellow-parliamentarians were in fact concerned as much with the need for social order as with the desire for political liberty. They feared the prospect of mob rule, the tyranny of the multitude, as well as the tyranny of the King; and although their approach to the origins and nature of power was novel, the conclusions they drew about the role of the people were far from democratic. Only a few pamphleteers in the early 1640s did explore the possibility that the 'people' might have to rebel against a corrupt parliament (the Scot Samuel Rutherford was one), and on the whole there was a reluctance to pursue the topic of the positive political rights of those outside the elite.

More likely to arouse a sense of genuine popular involvement in the struggle against the King were those calls to resistance based on religious, especially biblical, arguments. Parker's theories were not of course truly secular (he accepted that whereas man is the author of political power, 'the Law is the Instrument, and God is the establisher of both'), but his type of argument needs to be distinguished from the more explicit call to arms based on scriptural warrant which played a crucial role in mobilizing support for the armies of parliament. Puritan preachers played an inestimable part in trying to convince the nation that the cause of parliament was the cause of God. Special sermons to be preached on fast-days were commissioned by parliament and publicly circulated. These quoted texts, such as the famous passage on the curse of Meroz in the book of Judges 23, which justified resistance to an ungodly ruler. Efforts were also made to show that even those passages which had previously been used to point out the sinfulness of rebellion (for example, Romans 13) could, on closer inspection, be interpreted in a light favourable to parliament. Such morale-raising ventures of necessity stressed the role of the common people in war, with the Independent preacher Jeremiah Burroughes in 1643 going so far as to exhort even women to aid the cause by encouraging their sons and husbands to join the army (Greaves and Zaller, 1982). Burroughes, in fact, was one of those small band of writers prepared to admit that there might be circumstances in which people would be justified in resisting a corrupt parliament. Millenarian tracts (that is, those which portrayed the war as a struggle against Antichrist which would usher in the 1000-year reign of the saints on earth) were often particularly explicit about the vital role to be played by ordinary people, even the poor, in the resistance. This democratic emphasis in the call to the godly was to prove an important seedbed for later more radical religious ideas (see chapter 4).

The arguments which parliament had used to justify resistance to the King were pressed into further service to vindicate his trial and execution and to defend the legitimacy of the infant Republic. The notions of popular consent and parliamentary sovereignty, skilfully deployed, could be used to confirm the supporters of parliament in their belief that it was their duty to obey the new regime, but they were likely to be less compelling to those conservative Presbyterians and royalists who had bound themselves to uphold monarchy. To convince the latter that the Republic might command the obedience of the subject, new polemical weapons were also employed which focused on the purpose of government rather than its origin, and relied for their force on a blurring of the distinction between 'might' and 'right.' However, just as parliament's original defence of its actions had drawn on a variety of arguments from different sources and lacked real intellectual coherence, so too the defence of the Republic was often an eclectic mixture involving notions of law, history and scripture.

The charge against the King and the details of the sentence passed upon him stressed the idea that the King had been entrusted with his office and had been bound by oath to protect the interests of the people whose welfare was the purpose of government. In exercising his authority he had been limited by the laws of the land. Charles Stuart, however, had abused this trust and overstepped these laws. Therefore the people, represented in parliament, were justified in calling him to account. Morality, too, demanded action against Charles who had wilfully refused to accept God's judgement on his cause and instead had shed the innocent blood of his subjects by fomenting fresh military action in 1648. The validity of parliament's actions was further asserted by strenuous declarations of 'parliamentary' supremacy ('parliamentary' now being taken to refer to the Commons alone). On 4 January 1649 the House of Commons passed a resolution which declared that whatever they resolved had the force of law, even without the agreement of the King or House of Lords. 'The Commons of England in Parliament assembled', they announced, 'do declare that the people are, under God, the original of all just power: And also declare that the Commons of England in Parliament assembled, being chosen by and representing the people, have the supreme power in this nation' (A. Sharp, 1983, p. 232).

On 22 March 1649 there followed an official defence of the Rump Parliament's policy. Two thousand copies of this document were ordered to be printed for distribution to the localities, and for the benefit of foreign powers, on whose opinion the external security of the regime depended, translations were made into Latin, French and Dutch. The document began with an affirmation of the original power of the people: 'the first institution of the office of King in this nation was by agreement of the people', and made reference to the primary end of 'the good of the nation'. But many other species of argument were also adduced. The declaration took on its critics who, it said, might wish to cite scriptural warrant for the divine right of kings. Monarchy is not the only divinely ordained form of government, the Rump countered, echoing many statements made during the years of civil war. 'For the phrase "anointed", no learned divine will affirm it to be applicable to the Kings of England as to those of Judah and Israel, or more to a King than to every other magistrate or servant of God . . .' In addition, the declaration appealed to natural law to support the rights of the people, and to English history to demonstrate the existence of Anglo-Saxon freedoms before the Norman Conquest. The antiquity of the laws of England was also mentioned, as was the model of present experience which, the Rump declared, showed that free (non-monarchical) states could flourish at the present time (A. Sharp, 1983).

Such a *mélange* of ideas with nods in the direction of both radicalism and traditionalism illustrates perhaps the Rump's essentially defensive mentality in 1649. Far from wishing to forge ahead to found a new political and social order, it was content with a more cautious balancing act, wishing neither to dash completely the hopes of its more radical supporters nor to fuel the fears of its conservative foes. A similar eclecticism was displayed by other government propagandists including John Milton, whose *The Tenure of Kings and Magistrates* was published in February 1649 and reissued a year later. Milton argued squarely for the people's right to depose and punish unjust kings and grounded his case on a whole gamut of authorities, including natural law, biblical sanctions for tyrannicide, as well as plain common-sense. 'No man who knows aught', averred Milton, 'can be so stupid to deny that all men naturally were borne free' (quoted in Erskine-Hill and Storey, 1983, p. 121).

Arguments based on the consent of the people and/or the sovereignty of parliament were therefore an important, if not the only, element in the defence of the new Republic. In their approach to the origins of government and the legitimacy of rulers they marked an important break with tradition, although more traditional arguments continued to be heard. They also provided an ideological bridge between the parliamentarians and the Levellers, for the latter's programme had as its starting-point the belief that government was grounded in the will of the people. However, two things distinguished this so-called 'Independent' position from its more left-

21

wing critics. First, it was not principally concerned with the setting-up of a new constitution or with arguing about the ideal form of government. Second, it was not concerned to justify a truly democratic political or social order by translating its belief in the original power of the people into active political rights for the middling and lower orders as a whole. On the contrary, the 'Independent' notion of political power remained somewhat elitist in tone. The emphasis, as with Henry Parker earlier, was on the people acting not by and for themselves but through the medium of their elected representatives. In this way the concern for liberty could be reconciled with the need for order, but it was not a position which was calculated to win the support of the Leveller movement which the army and their Independent allies would soon be forced to crush.

On the other hand, these ideas were still too radical to appeal to Presbyterians and former royalists whose allegiance was necessary if the regime was to continue on a sound and stable footing. Another theory of political obligation had to be found which would legitimize obedience to the Republic for men who had previously sworn to uphold kingship, as the Presbyterians had done in the Solemn League and Covenant of 1643. This problem became particularly acute when the Rump Parliament decided that before 20 February 1650 all adult males should be compelled to subscribe an 'Engagement' to be faithful to the Commonwealth of England 'as it is now established, without a King or House of Lords'. How could this test of political citizenship be made acceptable to those who had taken an oath to uphold monarchy? One answer to this problem lay in the arguments of a group of writers whom Quentin Skinner has called 'the *de facto* theorists' (1972). The *de facto* defence of the Commonwealth, which concentrated on the government's practical ability, as a matter of fact, to maintain order and enforce obedience, rather than on its moral right to do so, drew on both religious and secular ideas. Not all writers were intellectually rigorous enough to separate these strands, and appeals to submit to God's providence (a recurrent theme in the religious strand) were very often mixed with arguments based on the needs of political society (the keystone of the secular case). While the religious arguments based on Scripture merely turned the pre-Civil War case for non-resistance neatly on its head, the secular considerations fundamentally revised traditional assumptions about the origins and nature of power. This develop-ment reached its radical apotheosis in the work of Thomas Hobbes, whom Quentin Skinner has persuaded us should be placed in the ideological context of the *de facto* theorists (1972).

Among those theorists who addressed the problem of obedience from a religious standpoint were John Dury, Francis Rous and Anthony Ascham, although Ascham in particular was more notable for his secular arguments. They concentrated not on the lawfulness of the government as such, but on the subject's duty to obey it. Dury employed Calvinistic arguments to prove that subjects should not 'intermeddle' in affairs of state or presume to judge the 'great ones of the world'; Ascham recommended that Englishmen should merely accept that 'the King of Kings hath chang'd our Vice-Roys'; while Rous tackled the problem from the standpoint of that much studied text from Romans 13. Rous's argument boiled down to the contention that what St Paul had really meant in his epistle to the Romans was 'we must obey *whatever* powers are in a position to command obedience' since those in power, whatever their origins, must occupy that position as a result of God's will and providence. 'For if any man do excel in power', he argued, 'it is now out of doubt that he received that power of God. Wherefore without all exception thou must yield thyself up to him and heartily obey him' (Skinner, 1972, p. 83). Rous's interpretation was soon demolished by his critics, although invocations of providence continued to be made even by those who adopted other, more secular, arguments.

Of the 'secular' theorists, Anthony Ascham and Marchamont Nedham deserve especial note. Ascham, whose ideas had been influenced by European thinkers including Hugo Grotius, started off by making a distinction between 'right' and 'power', and was concerned primarily with the latter. He and other *de facto* theorists were in effect prepared to concede and indeed to prove that a new government might be lawfully obeyed even though in itself it was not a lawful power. Those who followed in Ascham's footsteps progressively weakened the distinction between 'right' and 'power' to the point where they could claim with Nedham that 'it is undeniably evident that the present prevailing party in England have a right and just title to be our governors' (Skinner, 1972, p. 93). Their mode of argument had at its centre not the origins of government but its purpose. Ascham argued that the end of government was the protection of the lives and estates of its inhabitants; any government which ensured that protection deserved the obedience of its citizens, for the alternative was simply to lapse into internecine war. Hence he contended that those who had full possession of power might be granted the right to rule because they were able to control the means of human preservation. Conversely, he argued, the right of self-preservation which inheres in all men justifies them in obeying such power.

Marchamont Nedham, one of the most skilled of government publicists, took Ascham's argument further in *The Case of the*

Commonwealth of England, Stated (1650). Nedham had had a rather chequered career, having edited both royalist and parliamentarian papers. It was probably to secure his freedom from gaol that he agreed to write for the Commonwealth in 1649, and thereafter from his position as editor of the Rump's official newsbook, *Mercurius Politicus*, he was ideally placed to propagate *de facto* notions to a wide public. Large sections from *The Case* were used as front-page editorials for about a year after September 1650. Nedham's chapter headings succinctly expressed his argument: 'That the power of the Sword Is, and Ever Hath Been, the Foundation of All Titles to Government'; 'That Non-submission to Government Justly Deprives Men of the benefit of Its Protection'; and 'That a Government Erected by a Prevailing Part of the People Is As Valid *de iure* As If It Had the Ratifying Consent of the Whole' (Knachel, 1969).

Several *de facto* writers, including Ascham, Nedham, Albertus Warren and Francis Osborne, eventually recognized in the works of Thomas Hobbes a theory of political obligation very similar to their own. Hobbes in turn was aware of these similarities and wanted in his writing to present an argument which would settle the disorders of the time. His method of argument (but not his conclusions) were strikingly innovative and radical since they cut across all traditional assumptions about arguing the basis of legitimacy. His method of reasoning, unique among the *de facto* theorists, was based on geometry, and it applied to the study of human nature and civil society some of the most advanced concepts of the physical sciences, particularly those relating to matter and motion. Having proved that self-preservation is the first law of nature, Hobbes went on to explore in company with these other writers 'the mutual relation between protection and obedience' (Skinner, 1972, p. 97). Hobbes believed that only an absolute sovereign power within the state could guarantee that protection for its citizens which it was the purpose of government to provide. So long as government maintained this protection, it was the duty of the subject to obey, saving only his right to preserve his own life. Only when government failed to provide protection was disobedience or resistance justified. Hobbes's sovereign power was to be absolute and indivisible, and it could be consistent with either a monarchical or parliamentary system of government. It followed that in Hobbes's ideal state active political participation would be at a discount. Hobbes in fact was in favour of withdrawal from politics, and believed that meddling in public matters would lead the citizen to neglect his private affairs. He did not approve of 'that liberty which the lower sort of citizens, under pretence of religion, do challenge to themselves', and he was hostile to the Levellers who he believed where in favour of the expropriation of land (K. Thomas, 1965). Hobbes's views, therefore, were neither liberal nor democratic. He was concerned with the need for order rather than with the maintenance of liberty or just rights. He was preoccupied with submission and obedience, not with the consent of the people or the accountability of rulers. His theories propounded the duty of obedience to government as such, not specifically to that government which ruled in England in the early 1650s. His thought therefore needs to be set in a much wider perspective than the ideological debate on the English Revolution, but its similarities to that of the defenders of the Republic deserve to be noted none the less.

A Free Commonwealth?

Many of the *de facto* theorists had not had as an essential part of their argument the defence of republicanism as such. To Ascham, for example, forms of government were in themselves of little significance, although the more overtly republican Nedham had put greater emphasis on the 'excellency of a free state' and the disadvantages of monarchy. There were other republican groups, however, for whom the defence of the republican form was a more explicit objective, and for whom any kind of government by a single person was perceived as fatal to liberty. Not surprisingly, many men of this persuasion became ardent critics of Cromwell's power under the Protectorate, and the arguments they put forward appealed to some dissident elements in the army and to former members of the Rump. In 1659 their views were thrust into prominence once more when parliament and the army again contended for power in the state. This brand of republicanism, whose supporters are often called Commonwealthmen, has to be distinguished from that of political radicals like the Levellers. Although some Commonwealthmen had links with lower-class radical groups outside parliament, their ideology was in the main concerned with the limitation of executive power and the prevention of tyranny; they were therefore principally concerned with the redistribution of power among institutions, not among social classes. However, some of them, including the political theorist James Harrington, envisaged the setting up of a more liberal political order in which there would have been an extension of active political rights beyond the elite. Moreover, most republicans also supported widespread religious toleration.

Republicans could arrive at their beliefs by different routes and could take different views of what an ideal republic should be. Prominent members of the Rump, like Arthur Hesilrige and Thomas

Scot, remained convinced of the merits of that institution after its dissolution in 1653, opposed the Protectorate and tried to obstruct its legislative programme, and worked for the recall of the Rump in 1659. They wanted a sovereign, preferably single-chamber, legislature, independent of and capable of controlling the executive, which would reflect the will of the people. Some republicans were predominantly influenced by religious ideals, attaching millenarian significance to the notion of a republic, like the Fifth Monarchists, and believing, as did Sir Henry Vane, that the civil liberty of a republic would go hand-in-hand with liberty of conscience. Others were more influenced by classical models, looking back to the wisdom of the ancients for their inspiration. These 'classical republicans', on whom we shall concentrate in this section, included men like Thomas Challoner, Henry Nevile and Henry Marten who sat in Interregnum parliaments and were active in political debate, and intellectuals like John Milton and James Harrington, each of whom owed much to classical inspiration but also transcended its bounds. On the whole, classical republicans did not attract a popular following, but especially in 1659 their ideas were seized on as possible solutions to political instability. In that year Harrington's proposals were promoted in pamphlets and petitions and discussed in political clubs like that in Bow Street, Covent Garden, and in the famous Rota Club founded in the autumn. It would not be wise, however, to draw too sharp a distinction between 'puritan republicans' and 'classical republicans'. Both Milton and Harrington, for example, drew on various intellectual traditions: Milton was a great Christian humanist who was influenced by both the Bible and the legacy of antiquity, while Harrington betrayed millenarian enthusiasm as well as respect for ancient wisdom. Nor did respect for classicism mean indifference to religious problems. Most men who were influenced by classical models did not fit easily into the Puritan mould, but they were as committed to religious toleration as many sectarian radicals.

For some men classical republicanism was 'a language not a programme' (Worden, 1981, p. 193). Classical learning gave them a way of looking at political problems or an intellectual reference-point, rather than a blueprint for the future. Others believed that more direct political lessons could be learned by examining the examples of Rome and Sparta, where 'ancient prudence' reigned and whose spiritual affinities with the English Republic they now stressed. They admired writers like Polybius, Tacitus and Livy and studied them not merely at first hand but through their Renaissance interpreters, especially Machiavelli. Machiavelli's *Discourses on Livy* was much consulted for its views on corruption. In their own day these republicans admired Venice which they saw as a living example of republican virtue, superior in some respects even to the 'ancient prudence' of Rome and Sparta. Central to their political creed was a belief in reason. They saw politics as a conflict between reason on the one hand, and passion and will on the other. They believed that whereas hereditary monarchy would embody passion and will, popular sovereignty would answer to reason. This rationalism, which Worden rightly describes as a secularizing force in politics, was very far removed from the divine right principles on which the Stuart monarchy had been founded. So too their belief that all power derives originally from the people, and can in certain circumstances be resumed by the people, points away from the political theories current in Stuart England.

But in one significant respect the beliefs of these republicans had affinities with the views expressed by Charles I in 1642: this was in the crucial importance they attached to 'mixture' in government and the balance of elements in the state. Like Charles and those exponents of the theory of a mixed state before him, they believed that there were three 'pure' or simple forms of government – monarchy, aristocracy and democracy – all of which possessed certain virtues, but each of which on its own would degenerate into instability and inconvenience, in the form of tyranny, oligarchy and anarchy respectively. If, however, these three 'pure' elements were to be combined or mixed and a balance or equilibrium achieved among them, then stability and permanence would be secured. Where the classical republicans of the 1650s differed fundamentally from the theorists of mixed monarchy was in their belief that the best form of government had to be a republic in which the executive element was not represented by a hereditary monarch.

Their notion of balance also led them to conclusions about the distribution of power among institutions in the state which were quite different from those of Charles. Whereas Charles, and indeed Philip Hunton, had attributed the functions of monarchy, aristocracy and democracy to King, Lords and Commons respectively, the republicans considered parliament to be the 'aristocratic' element and the people themselves the 'democratic' element. But opinion was divided among republicans (as it had been among classical and Renaissance writers) on whether the 'aristocratic' or the 'democratic' (or popular) element in the state should be dominant. The Harringtonian compromise, espoused by other writers too, was to accept that whereas power originated in the popular element, in the actual administration of the state the 'aristocratic' element should prevail. In effect, classical republicans stressed that the people had delegated their power to the other elements in the state. They did,

27

however, admit that power could be repossessed by the people, and so conceded a popular right of resistance, but this did not mean that they condoned the prospect of democratic uprisings or held flattering opinions about the political judgement of the masses. Milton, for one, spoke slightingly of the opinions of the lower classes, and was particularly disgusted at the favourable popular reception accorded to the royalist apologia *Eikon Basilike*. Yet it must be emphasized that although the classical republicans did not believe that power should pass out of the hands of the propertied classes, they did not simply mean when they spoke of the 'aristocracy' the peerage or gentry of their day. Harrington's 'nobility' in his ideal state might constitute a third of the population, while the fountainhead of Milton's 'aristocracy' was the middling sort of people. Classical republicans also believed that those engaged in public service should show certain qualities of virtue and public spirit. These qualities were not merely those attributable to birth and estate, but included patriotism, valour, independence and other characteristics which some writers imbued with Puritan overtones of honesty and godliness (Fink, 1945; Pocock, 1957; Zagorin, 1954).

Undoubtedly the classical republican of greatest intellectual stature was James Harrington. In his blueprint for an ideal commonwealth, *The Commonwealth of Oceana* published in 1656, and in his later pamphlets he set out not only a novel plan for the institutions of government, but a new theory of political power and a new theory of historical change (Pocock, 1957). Like Thomas Hobbes, therefore, Harrington's most radical contribution to political thought lay in his basic analytical method. Briefly, Harrington believed that historically the balance of property had always determined the balance of power in the state. But when the institutions of the state failed to reflect that balance of property and power, conflict and instability inevitably resulted. Harrington's grasp of the relationship between property and power was not, however, proto-Marxist; it was based on no real sense of economics or economic relationships as such. Instead, Harrington believed that property determined political power because it first of all determined military power; the distribution of land dictated whether the soldier should fight as a citizen for the state or as a dependent for his feudal patron or lord. In turn,\ the nature of military tenures would decide the nature of the state.

In his own time Harrington believed that with the help of an agrarian law to prevent the concentration of too much property in too few hands, the triumph of the English freeholder could usher in a new age of 'ancient prudence' in which the state would be defended by a citizen militia and political stability would be permanently achieved. Harrington proposed that no man should hold land worth more than £2,000; this would ensure at least 5,000 landowners and probably more. The type of military service owed to the state would be related to the amount of land held: men worth more than £200 per annum would serve in the mounted militia, those with less in the foot. Each would have different types of political rights, while servants would not participate in politics at all. Harrington proposed a two-chamber legislative assembly (a point of contrast with other republicans, as was his contempt for the Rump as a distasteful oligarchy). He desired a senate of 300 men, drawn from those who served in the mounted militia, which could initiate and debate laws; and an assembly of 1,000 men, representing both the more popular element and those with land worth more than £100 per annum in the ratio of four to three, which could merely accept or reject these laws without debate. This careful system of checks and balances would have been very difficult to operate in practice, but it did betoken a willingness to diffuse some political power among the middling sort. As Austin Woolrych has pointed out, 'few men worth less than £100 a year can have played *any* direct part in legislation in Harrington's lifetime, or for long before and after it' (1980, p. 63). Other parts of Harrington's plan provided for the rotation of officeholders, secret ballots, liberty of conscience as well as a national religion, and a global foreign policy which would extend liberty of conscience and civil liberty to the world (Pocock, 1957, 1977).

Harrington's particular remedy for the ills of his time was unique, but his and other republicans' concern to maintain a bulwark against tyranny in the shape of a refashioned balanced polity marked a liberal advance in thinking about the origins of power, the accountability of rulers and the political rights of the people. Their solutions, however, were far from being truly democratic or egalitarian. They would probably have been prepared to translate their belief in the ultimate sovereignty of the people into positive political rights for at least some of the middling sort, but their concept of the 'people' was unlikely to embrace the poor. They might have extended the franchise beyond the limit set in the Instrument of Government (the constitution of the Protectorate published in December 1653) of £200 a year in real or personal estate, but yet they did not seem to envisage even the 'better sort' of people playing an active and continuing role in deciding day-to-day public affairs. Nor were they concerned with the wide range of social and economic issues which affected the daily lives of the 'poorer sort'. They were, therefore, in all these respects markedly less radical than the Levellers, to whom we now turn.

3 The Levellers

In recent times the Levellers have enjoyed a diminishing reputation among historians of seventeenth-century England. Once hailed as the champions of a democratic revolution who were defeated only by the political turncoats in the New Model Army, and still referred to by some present-day politicans as the founding fathers of the working-class movement, the Levellers have been severely cut down to size by the current triumph of the revisionists. Their significance in the English Revolution, it is now claimed, has been seriously overestimated by writers such as H. N. Brailsford and Christopher Hill. Marxist as well as conservative historians would now question the extent of their support, their impact on events (especially in the heady days of the army revolt in 1647), and the true nature of their apparently radical and democratic programme. None the less, despite the reservations about the movement which many historians now share, it is hard to deny that, in comparison with the parliamentarians and republicans whom we have examined so far, the Levellers broke new ground in several ways. They went farther than other groups in tackling the problem of building a new constitution instead of merely tinkering with the balance of institutions in the old. They sought to extend active political rights well beyond the charmed circle of the elite, and to develop new mechanisms for enforcing the accountability of the governors to the governed. They grounded their programme on a new ideological basis by developing arguments based on the doctrines of natural rights and of popular sovereignty. And they mobilized support for their movement by employing sophisticated modern techniques of propaganda and organization.

Disagreement among historians on the essential nature of the movement has been compounded by ambiguities in its composition and in its ideology, which in turn spring from the circumstances in which the Leveller party was formed and the way in which its policy was formulated. Rising out of the immediate political and religious turmoil of 1646–9, but tapping also longer-term social and economic grievances, the Leveller movement throve on the very fact that it had a multi-faceted appeal and could for a brief period represent many things to many men. Both ideologically and socially it was, as the Baptist Henry Denne described it, a very heterogeneous body. Its rapid rise and fall, its relatively short life, the fact that the leaders and their followers were thrown together by the crisis of the moment, all this meant that intellectual coherence suffered at the hands of an urgent need to hammer out a programme. The Levellers were not like a revolutionary party which had had a long period in opposition or in exile during which to assimilate and integrate various strands in its political thinking. Some historians have chosen to see a fundamental distinction between, on the one hand, those allegedly more moderate or 'constitutional' Levellers who concentrated on political reform and were less interested in social and economic restructuring and, on the other hand, the more radical wing of the movement, the 'true Levellers', which concerned itself with social democracy and economic problems and which had real affinities with the Diggers (Hill, 1975). This distinction seems much too arbitrary, and tends to obscure the rather more confused reality of the Leveller movement, where there was great internal flux and issues were seized upon and then abandoned as the political climate demanded. Changing external circumstances, especially relations with the New Model Army, dictated that policies (for example, on the franchise) should be modified and altered on grounds of expediency; and the individual concerns of particular leaders (such as Lilburne's interest in London's affairs or Overton's concern with social problems) might lead to specific issues being aired for a time without being fully and clearly integrated into the main platform. Policy documents designed to enlist mass support – the major petitions to parliament in March 1647 and September 1648 and the three Agreements of the People in November 1647, December 1648 and May 1649, for example – are a sure guide to the Leveller programme, but are not necessarily the fullest statements of Leveller views. To these must be added the writings of a veritable host of prominent figures in the movement: Lilburne himself was the author of eighty pamphlets, and Richard Overton wrote forty between September 1645 and July 1649 alone (Greaves and Zaller, 1983).

The embarrassment of riches which this vast outpouring of pamphlet literature presents to the student of Leveller ideology raises a further difficulty about the composition and membership of the movement. The presentation of such a wide range of issues, together with the mass propagandist techniques which were used to procure subscriptions to petitions and a large turn-out at demonstrations, makes it tempting to overestimate the strength of the party as such. As we shall see, expressions of sympathy with the attitudes the Levellers struck were numerous and vocal, especially in parts of London and the south-east, but it is not certain that this generalized sympathy was translated into widespread committed, consistent and sustained support for all the details of the party programme. Even in London, active party membership was probably much smaller than the numbers who turned out to Leveller spectacles, such as Lilburne's trial or Rainsborough's funeral, would suggest. Identification with the grievances the Levellers articulated was undoubtedly more widespread than active support for the remedies they espoused. Conservative historians would particularly demur at the suggestion that the radical ideology of the Leveller leaders was typical even of those social groups from which most support for the movement came. Clubmen, not Levellers (or Diggers), were arguably the true representatives of the wishes of the middling sort (see chapter 5). The Levellers' failure to build up solid grass-roots commitment to the party and its official programme outside a limited section of the population of the south-east was, as we shall see, one of the main reasons for the downfall of the movement.

None the less, the difficulty of determining the nature of the Leveller programme or the extent of its support should not blind us to an appreciation of just how remarkable a phenomenon the Leveller movement of mid-seventeenth-century England was. 'Nowhere else', G.E. Aylmer writes, 'before the 1760s, or even perhaps before 1789, do we find the combination of radical journalism and pamphleteering, ideological zeal, political activism, and mass organization that prevailed in England from 1646 to 1649' (Aylmer, 1975, p. 9).

Origins and Influences

In explaining the background to and the origins of the Leveller movement we can look at three main sets of factors. First, there were particular grievances which the Levellers could exploit and which provided them with the issues on which to focus: these grievances encompassed both long- and short-term economic and social factors, the exceptional political conditions of the mid-1640s, and the religious disputes into which the nation had been plunged by the dismantling of episcopacy. Secondly, there was the intellectual heritage on which the Levellers could draw to establish the ideological underpinning for their programme of reform: this included the legacy of radical Protestantism; the doctrines of natural law and popular consent, which were ripe for extension into theories of natural rights and popular sovereignty; and particular interpretations of the course of English history since 1066. And third, there were models of popular participation, examples drawn from the actual political and religious experiences of Leveller leaders and supporters, which could inspire the party as it strove to develop practical solutions to the ills of the time.

The socio-economic preconditions for the rise of a movement like the Levellers had been created by long-term changes in landholding and in manufacturing. Those changes which had adversely affected the status and prosperity of the urban and rural 'middling sort of people' were especially important in providing potential supporters for the Levellers, who were to become principally the spokesmen for the 'industrious sort'. Pressure on the smaller peasant farmer who lacked the resources of his larger neighbour to benefit from an expanding market and rising prices; the discontent of the insecure copyholder subject to rack-renting; and the fear of the small cottager or husbandman at the prospect of enclosure, produced dissatisfaction which the Levellers could tap and issues on which they could take a stand. Of even greater significance were the problems of the small craftsmen and tradesmen, particularly in the towns, whose independence seemed threatened by large-scale merchants and entrepreneurs. The existence of such problems in London was crucially important, for the capital was to provide the core of the Leveller movement. Here a large pool of discontent existed among journeymen unable, because of changes in the structure of manufacturing, to find the resources to set up as masters in their own right. Anger smouldered among small tradesmen and merchants chafing at the alleged oppression of the guilds, the livery companies and, above all, the Merchant Adventurers; and indignation reigned among all those London householders who felt their economic rights and political interests threatened by corruption and oligarchy in the municipal government itself.

Many of these long-term economic grievances were felt throughout the early seventeenth century, but discontent was seriously exacerbated by the particular distress of the years from 1646 to 1649. The dislocations of war had seriously disrupted trade, unemployment increased, prices rose but wages failed to keep pace and at the end of the decade harvests were extremely poor. To add to this distress, parliament's imposition of taxes to pay for the army, especially the hated excise, had raised the price of consumable goods even further, again to the particular annoyance of the London tradesmen. In January 1648 a pro-Leveller pamphlet entitled *The Mournfull Cryes of many thousand poor Tradesmen, who are ready to famish through decay of Trade* gave vent to this collection of grievances:

Its your Taxes, Customs, and Excize, that compells the Countrey to raise the price of food, and to buy nothing from us but meer absolute necessaries; and then you of the City that buy our Work, must have your Tables furnished, and your Cups overflow; and therefore will give us little or nothing for our Work, even what you please, because you know we must sell for moneys to set our Families on work, or else we famish: Thus our Flesh is that whereupon you Rich men live, and wherewith you deck and adorn yourselves. (quoted in Shaw, 1968, p. 118)

London was, therefore, important to the Levellers because it was the scene of much economic distress for the small trader and artisan, but it was also significant because it was the focus of political and religious debate.

By 1646 the fighting in the Civil War had ended, but peace brought its problems no less profound than war. Between 1646 and 1649 the fundamental question of what to do with the King and what sort of political settlement to erect in the wake of parliamentary victories had to be resolved. An important consideration in all this was not simply how to preserve the gains made against the King, but also how to reach a settlement which would justify the sacrifices of ordinary people. Fears that these gains and sacrifices might be abandoned by parliament formed an essential backdrop to Leveller activities. As a developing issue, the quest for a settlement, coupled with radical suspicions of parliament's intentions, played a key part in determining the Levellers' relations with the officers and soldiers of the New Model Army. These relations in turn were crucial in determining how much influence the Levellers could exercise on the course of political events. In time it was to become very clear, not least in the Putney Debates of October–November 1647 and the Whitehall Debates of December 1648, that the Levellers and the Grandees (or senior officers) of the army differed on the nature of the political and religious settlement that should be reached with the King, and on the distribution of political power that should obtain in the new order. But in the immediate aftermath of the war it was also clear that both sides had good reason to fear and distrust the intentions of the dominant Presbyterian faction in parliament, that they shared a belief that a generous, compromise agreement should not be concluded with the King, and that by mid-1647 the Levellers had recognized that the army should have a large say in shaping the eventual settlement. The possibility of collaboration between the Levellers and the army Grandees would probably not have been seriously mooted, however, had it not been that the grievances and aspirations of the Levellers found such echoes among the rank and file that the Grandees had to take note in order to preserve the discipline and unity of the army. The radicalization of sections of the rank and file did not happen solely, or even directly, because of Leveller influence; it happened because the soldiers' perception of their own ill-treatment at the hands of the Presbyterian majority produced a political consciousness on which the Levellers could capitalize. The Levellers thus acted as a catalyst in forcing the soldiers to recognize and articulate their own role in producing a political settlement, but they were never powerful enough to make the Grandees dance entirely to the Leveller tune (Kishlansky, 1979a, 1979b). However, the Presbyterians' treatment of the army had provided the Levellers with an additional issue to exploit, an extra source of support on which to draw, and a lever with which to propel themselves into the political spotlight.

Integral to the confused politics of 1646–9 was the fact that a religious settlement also had to be hammered out in the wake of the destruction of episcopacy. In 1646 this issue came to a head when parliament prepared to erect a presbyterian system of church government. This attempt to set up a national church, to preserve the links between church and state and to impose discipline and unity on the godly, spurred into action those who wished to see a more tolerant system developed, with freedom for separatist churches and a loosening of the bonds between church and state. Many future Leveller supporters and leaders had already become convinced of the case for religious toleration in the early 1640s, and their desire to advance this cause was a key factor in the formation of the Leveller movement. The relationship between political and religious radicalism was very close, especially in London. Many separatist congregations or gathered churches had been formed in the very suburbs of the city where craftsmen and traders of the middling sort were suffering under the prevailing economic conditions. Each of the major Leveller spokesmen, including Richard Overton, William Walwyn and John Lilburne, had been involved in the struggle for religious freedom and had several years of pamphleteering and agitation behind them before they came together as a group in 1645. Religious toleration was a major issue in the Leveller campaign and occupied a vital position in their programme throughout the life of the party. The movement was crucially dependent for its strength on support from the gathered churches, and its appeal to radical elements in the army was likewise based in part on shared beliefs in toleration and liberty of conscience. In some ways the Leveller policy of political and social reform 'amounted to an expression of the aspirations of the sectarian community at large' (Tolmie, 1977, p.

149). Although the withdrawal of much sectarian support was eventually to cripple the Leveller movement, in its early days the large coincidence of views and the overlap in personnel between Levellers and religious radicals was crucially important in promoting and shaping the party.

Economic and social distress, concern over the political settlement with the King, and anxiety about the imposition of an oppressive religious system, provided both the context for the emergence of the Leveller movement and the issues on which its programme could focus. But the definition and elaboration of that programme did not only depend on the immediate practical concerns of its supporters. Its ideological content and its political language reflected the intellectual heritage of the leaders of the movement. Leveller ideology was based on three principal sets of ideas. Each of these had been prefigured in the parliamentarian ideology we examined in chapter 2, but whereas the parliamentarians had interpreted these notions in a restrictive, conservative manner, the Levellers developed and extended them in a liberal, radical and democratic direction.

The first major strand in Leveller thinking was the influence of radical Protestantism, which some writers would wish to define more narrowly as the influence of Calvinistic Puritanism. Certainly the Levellers owed a great debt to Puritanism, but by 1646 their leaders and many of their supporters had abandoned an orthodox Calvinist position. None the less some Calvinist notions were eminently transferrable, psychologically as much as theologically, from the religious to the secular sphere, and the ambiguities inherent in Calvinism could be exploited in a variety of ways (Woodhouse, 1974). The doctrine of predestination, for example, with its distinction between the elect and the reprobate, might immediately suggest an elitist, hierarchical view of society, but in Leveller hands a stress on equality *within* the elect could be used to support more egalitarian notions. Similarly, the Puritan emphasis on inner spiritual worth and godly virtue suggested new criteria for the exercise of power: the challenge to traditional notions of leadership and rank could be transmuted into a demand for the monopoly of the elite on political power to be broken. The Puritan belief in a person's direct relationship with God and individual responsibility in biblical interpretation and other matters, linked to the intensely personal experience of knowledge of one's own salvation, undoubtedly influenced the highly individualistic temper of the Leveller movement. So too did the Puritan stress on activism, on the duty of the godly to act out God's purposes in the world, which encouraged a belief in the ability and right of the common people to control their own destiny through active political participation. Furthermore, the

36

voluntarist principle, which enjoined the godly to gather together in separate congregations, not only led to demands for religious toleration, but influenced the Levellers' concept of self-government.

The Levellers' propensity to develop the doctrines of radical Protestantism in a liberal direction was extended and reinforced by the second major influence on their thought: this was a cluster of ideas stemming from what G.E. Aylmer calls the 'rationalist, optimistic temper of the Renaissance, and more specifically the neo-classical idea of Natural Law' (1975, p. 12). The Levellers built on doctrines of natural law to produce a radical theory of the natural rights of man. The idea of 'natural law' (which had been used by Henry Parker) implied a set of principles implanted in nature by God which were knowable by and consonant with reason; since man himself was a rational creature he could discern these principles which, the Levellers now claimed, included certain natural rights. In 1646, in *The Free Man's Freedom Vindicated*, John Lilburne expressed this concept thus: 'All and every particular and individual man and woman, that ever breathed in the world, are by nature all equal and alike in their power, dignity, authority and majesty, none of them having (by nature) any authority, dominion or magisterial power one over and above another' (Shaw, 1968, p. 100).

The principle of reason and the belief in equal natural rights led the Levellers to espouse theories of popular consent and popular sovereignty (they believed in fact that only consent could give scope to reason). Hence also their emphasis on 'trust', that is their belief that those who governed did so on the basis of trust between themselves and the people to whom they were accountable. Where the Levellers differed radically from theorists like Henry Parker was in their insistence that sovereignty resided in the people and had not been delegated to parliament, and in their consequent desire to establish active political rights for the people and to restrict the powers of the legislature (Frank, 1955; Tuck, 1979; Woodhouse, 1974; Zagorin, 1954).

The third major intellectual influence on Leveller ideology was a set of ideas about English history and English law. Like the 'ancient constitution' theorists before them, the Levellers relied on a historical myth to defend their claim to be restoring chosen liberties, but in their case it was the rights of the people, not the privileges of parliament, which principally concerned them. Their attitudes here were in some ways highly ambivalent. On the one hand they appealed to Magna Carta, statute law and the principles of the common law to defend their claims about the legal rights of the individual, yet at the same time they subscribed to the historical myth of the 'Norman Yoke'. In their view, far from the principles of

37

the law and the constitution having been handed down in an unbroken line since time immemorial, the Norman Conquest of 1066 had marked a decisive break in English history: for them the Conquest represented the enslavement of a free English people and the repression of Anglo-Saxon representative institutions. They regarded the law itself as part of the Norman bondage, and despite appeals to Magna Carta and other enactments they believed the mainstream of the common law had been corrupted and that wide-ranging legal as well as political reform would be necessary to restore the lost rights and liberties of the people. Arguments based on the notion of lost liberties were not entirely consistent with those based on natural rights; the first argument focused on the recovery of rights which used to exist, the second on the pursuit of rights because they ought to exist (Hill, 1958). This reflects the transitional nature of much Leveller thinking, and their Janus-like use of extant political theories to point in new radical and even progressive directions.

The Levellers certainly did combine an appeal to history with an appeal to reason, but the emphasis lay most heavily on the latter. They had therefore moved away from using an adherence to tradition or a reliance on precedent as legitimizing arguments in themselves, and in their use of rationalist arguments they looked forward to Locke and Paine rather than back to the parliamentarians. Overall, indeed, the Levellers had made significant leaps forward in the development of a radical political ideology. It was a major advance to move from the spiritual equality of the elect to the equal political rights of saints and sinners alike, and from the rights of the godly to the liberties of all Englishmen, just as it was of crucial importance to progress from an appeal to precedent towards an appeal to reason. Perhaps not surprisingly, the Levellers do not always score highly in terms of logic and intellectual coherence. But as political activists and innovators, they pushed forward the frontiers of political debate, expressed the aspirations and grievances of sections of the population who had been ignored by many parliamentarian writers, and prefigured the radical agitators of the later eighteenth century.

It must also be remembered that the Leveller programme was the result not only of thought, but also of experience. This was certainly true of the leaders, especially John Lilburne. The issues on which the Levellers focused reflected almost exactly the problems of Lilburne's own career. Like John Wilkes in the 1760s, Lilburne managed to establish his personal history as a paradigm of national injustice and oppression. He had a boundless capacity for identifying his own sufferings with the cause of liberty: his tirades against the Merchant Adventurers' trading monopoly, the corruption of the government of

London, and arbitrary methods of trial and imprisonment reflected his own personal disasters as well as matters of general concern. In particular, he was able to use his repeated arrest and imprisonment by the authorities to generalize about oppression in a way which struck a responsive chord among his listeners, and provided a focus for agitation by the London crowd. Economic disaster, religious persecution and legal oppression: Lilburne had suffered them all. For this reason he was the ideal leader of a movement which reflected the grievances of the middling sort (Greaves and Zaller, 1983; Gregg, 1961).

Another type of experience also found its expression in the Leveller creed. The solutions they propounded to remedy their grievances were rooted in and inspired by actual models of popular participation. Many writers have noted that not merely the ideology of Puritanism but also the practice of the separatist churches influenced the Levellers in their ideal view of state and society: the actual experience of a small, relatively democratic and egalitarian religious community produced perhaps a more powerful image of society for many Leveller supporters than did intellectual theorizing. Likewise there were some practical precedents for political participation by the middling orders. Keith Thomas has drawn attention to the model of local government, with its opportunities for service as constable, churchwarden and juryman, and to the extension of the franchise to some of the middling sort before 1640, and has argued that such participation at 'village level' was 'a familiar enough experience to make its extension to the parliamentary sphere seem by no means unreasonable' (1972, p. 61). The expansion of the electorate in the early seventeenth century, the increase in contested elections in 1640, and the existence of a few constituencies like Westminster with a fairly broad franchise certainly meant that the Levellers' vision of wider political participation had something on which to build. But the most forceful model of popular action was surely the involvement of the common people in the Civil War: not merely their contribution to the fighting (although service in the New Model Army was clearly for some an energizing and radicalizing experience), but also their involvement with and influence upon political debate and decision-making, especially in London. It was not the Levellers but the parliamentarian preachers who first encouraged the belief that the common people should act out God's purposes and shift from a passive to an active role. It was not the Levellers who first brought the crowds on to the streets of London: there was precedent aplenty for the expression of popular opinion in the demonstrations outside parliament in 1641–2 and in the continuing pressure from all kinds of petitioners (including massive peace demonstrations) since the outbreak of war. Heightened political expectations and heightened political activity were as much the cause as the consequence of the formation of the Leveller movement in London; and it was in part to make sense of and ensure some gains from this degree of popular participation that the Leveller programme arose.

Beliefs and Programme

The Levellers' intellectual heritage combined with the fruits of practical experience to produce a political programme which had as its main theme a belief in the rights and liberties of the individual. Their concept of freedom, however, was cast in terms of 'freedom from restraint' as well as 'freedom to act'. Therefore, although they put forward positive claims for active political rights to be granted to the people, the thrust of many of their proposals had a more negative aspect. They certainly supported the liberty of the people, but this was cause and consequence of the fact that they were against the power of oligarchy and monopoly in government, in the economy, in the legal system and in religion. This combination of the positive and the negative was well expressed by Lilburne. In 1648 he wrote that those 'nicknamed Levellers are the supporters and true defenders of liberty and propriety, or anti-grandees, anti-imposters, anti-monopolists, anti-arbitrarians and anti-[economic]Levellers' (quoted in Greaves and Zaller, 1983).

The Levellers' political and constitutional proposals were designed to express their belief that government originated in a social contract, that the actions of government required the consent of the people, and that ultimate sovereignty resided in the people. They argued that in England in the later 1640s legitimate government had in effect been dissolved: parliament had so denied the liberties of the people that it had forfeited its right to govern. Therefore government (and indeed society) would have to be reconstituted by a new social contract. Hence the Levellers espoused an 'Agreement of the People' which all citizens would subscribe and which would both reconstitute political society and define the fundamental principles of the new political system (Frank, 1955; Zagorin, 1954). Those printed manifestos entitled on 'Agreement of the People' (published in November 1647, December 1648 and May 1649) are therefore to be construed literally: they were conceived as mechanisms for establishing the consent of the people to a new form of government which could ultimately be endorsed by all citizens. In setting out what that new form of government should be, whether in the Agreements themselves or in other declarations of policy, the Levellers addressed

40

themselves to two main questions. First, given the inherent sovereignty of the people, how could that sovereignty be actively and continuously expressed; and second, who exactly, for political purposes, were 'the people'? The first question was answered by designing a series of devices to ensure the accountability of parliament to the electorate, and by proposals to 'reserve' certain crucial powers to the people, to curtail executive power and to achieve a large measure of decentralization in government. The second problem, which was probably less important to Levellers than was the first, produced proposals for the extension of the franchise.

The Levellers wanted a parliament which could be made frequently and easily responsive to the popular will. For this reason they were hostile to the political power of the monarchy and the House of Lords, and were confirmed in this belief by their view that the King and the aristocracy had been the chief beneficiaries of that Norman Yoke which had been placed on the necks of the common people in 1066. Some Leveller writings did contain a theoretical defence of republicanism, and calls were clearly made for the abolition of monarchy and the House of Lords. Other spokesmen, however, were prepared to retain these institutions so long as neither had a 'negative voice' (or veto) over legislation. The real aim of policy on this issue was to ensure that popular sovereignty should be reflected, untrammelled by any other body, in a one-chamber assembly which exercised the sole legislative power in the state. To ensure the accountability of this assembly to the electorate, the Levellers also demanded frequent elections (either every one or every two years) and measures to reduce patronage and oligarchical influence both at elections and in the Commons itself. In this vein they wished to exclude lawyers from the Commons and to award MPs a modest salary to free them from economic dependence on rich patrons. A redistribution of parliamentary seats and an extension of the franchise would promote the same end.

These checks on the power of parliament were not deemed sufficient in themselves to translate the sovereignty of the people into a continuous political reality. The Levellers' experience gave them ample reason to be suspicious of men once they were in power and to fear the growth of corrupt, self-interested faction in the legislature. Their bitterness was vividly expressed in this *cri de coeur* in 1649: 'we have', they wrote 'by wofull experience found the prevalence of corrupt interests powerfully inclining most men once entrusted with authority, to pervert the same to their own domination, and to the prejudice of our Peace and Liberties' (quoted in Aylmer, 1975, p. 164). To counteract this they proposed that certain powers should be

41

forever 'reserved' to the people; that is, certain subjects were declared to be so fundamental to the liberties of the people that they were put beyond the normal legislative competence of parliament. How decisions could be taken on these subjects if the need arose was never clearly spelled out, but probably the Levellers envisaged that the people would voice an opinion through some sort of referendum. The number and nature of these reserved powers varied according to the circumstances in which the Levellers found themselves. There were only five in the first Agreement of the People in November 1647, including religious toleration and equality before the law, both of which remained fundamental to this part of the Leveller programme; but by the third Agreement in May 1649, the number of reserved powers had been considerably expanded to include other matters of a less important legal and fiscal nature.

The Levellers' antagonism to those who held the reins of power also led to a desire to limit the executive in their new system of government. This is most noticeable in their pronouncements in 1649, after they had been bitterly humiliated by the army Grandees. In late 1648 the Leveller leaders had been outwardly courted by Cromwell and Ireton and invited to talks at Whitehall, but after the execution of the King in January 1649 it was clear that they had outlived their usefulness to the army command and could be summarily disposed of. Realizing this, and believing that the new republican regime was no more a friend to liberty than the old, the Levellers published bitter attacks on their new masters in *Englands New Chains Discovered* (two parts, February and March 1649), and in *The Hunting of the Foxes* (21 March 1649). They were also led to make more explicit their hostility to executive power as such. The Levellers seem to have assumed that when parliament was actually sitting, it would exercise full executive authority, subject to the checks which would normally operate on the competence of the legislature. When parliament was not in session other arrangements would have to be made: either a Council of State would be formed which would include MPs, or else a committee of MPs would exercise authority 'limited and bounded with express instructions, and accountable to the next section [session]' (Shaw, 1968, p. 79). The Levellers were clearly concerned to prevent the concentration of power in a few hands, and therefore did not wish to have an executive either powerful in itself or with the independent resources to fill parliament with its own supporters.

In various ways, then, Leveller insistence on the sovereignty of the people had led them to rethink the details of the political structure at national level. But equally important to their belief in government by popular consent was their keen interest in the local structure of authority and the decentralization of power. Indeed, there is no doubt that the Levellers imagined that, once their new system was in operation, power in the provinces would be much more important than government at the centre. Their demand for the election of officeholders by local communities was therefore crucial: in this way, public officials could be made responsible and responsive to the popular will in communities small enough to make that democratic control effective. The Levellers' proposals here overlapped with their demands for legal and judicial reform, for, in common with general opinion, the administration of justice and the enforcement of the law was in their view a large part of the work of government (Manning, 1976). Hence the desire for locally elected judicial officals and locally based law courts. The Earnest Petition of January 1648 demanded that 'some chosen Representatives of every Parish proportionably may be the Electors of the Sheriffs, Justices of the Peace, Committee-men, Grand-jury men, and all ministers of Justice whatsoever' (Wolfe, 1944, p. 269). Decentralization was a consistent theme in many parts of the Leveller programme: it also influenced their demands for a locally trained and recruited militia in place of a centralized professional army, and it was reflected in their espousal of the independent rights of 'local' congregations. The revitalization of the small community – whether it be parish, borough, guild or church – was deemed essential to curb the power of oligarchy in law, politics, trade and religion. Decentralization was not merely as important as democracy: it was the indispensable condition for the democratization of the whole political system in church and state.

Among historians, Leveller plans for the devolution of power have received comparatively little emphasis compared with the close attention that has been given to the Leveller debate on the franchise. Despite various attempts to impose a spurious consistency on Leveller pronouncements on this subject, most writers would prefer simply to accept that the movement gave different answers at different times to the question 'who are the people?', and that there was always internal division on this issue. Therefore apparent shifts in opinion in the Levellers' public pronouncements are most usefully taken at face value. The logic of the Levellers' belief in the equal natural rights of every man and woman ought in theory to have impelled them towards the advocacy of universal suffrage. No one followed this path to the extent of calling for votes for women, but some Levellers clearly did demand universal *manhood* suffrage, although even this most radical group would have temporarily excluded men such as 'delinquents' (or former royalists). At the other end of the spectrum some moderate Levellers would have settled for a franchise restricted in the main to male heads of households owning modest amounts of property. In between, a case could be made for the exclusion of various types of working people. In *The Case of the Armie Truly Stated* (15 October 1647) Leveller influence in the army had produced the demand that 'all the freeborn at the age of 21 years and upwards, be the electors'. A few weeks later, however, when the Levellers came to debate the first Agreement of the People with the army Grandees at Putney, it was clear that there was a significant internal difference in the movement between those who believed that literally 'every man that is to live under a government ought first by his own consent to put himself under that government', and those who felt that only those 'that have not lost their birthright' ought to vote in elections (Woodhouse, 1974, p. 53). The notion of loss of birthright could open the way to some far-reaching exclusions from the franchise. The demands of political expediency and pressure from the Grandees also began to erode the case for universal manhood suffrage. In December 1648, in the second Agreement of the People (entitled *Foundations of Freedom*), the Levellers would have limited the franchise to 'Natives or Denizens of England, such as have subscribed this Agreement; not persons receiving Alms but such as are assessed ordinarily towards the relief of the poor; not servants to, or receiving wages from any particular person' (Wolfe, 1944, p. 297). This was a considerable, and perhaps untypical, retreat from the public position the Levellers had held in 1647, but by May 1649 the third Agreement restored the franchise to all men over 21 'not being servants, or receiving Alms, or having served the late King in Arms or voluntary Contributions' (Aylmer, 1975, p. 162).

The Marxist historian C.B. Macpherson has argued that even during the Putney Debates the Levellers wanted to deny the vote to all types of wage-earners and anyone who had ever had to rely on poor relief. He believes that the Levellers deemed a man to have lost his birthright when he alienated his labour, as all wage-earners, alms-takers, servants and beggars had done; and that when a man lost his birthright he forfeited his right to vote (1964). Keith Thomas, on the other hand, has argued more plausibly that the Levellers did not, on the whole, take the extreme view that to alienate one's labour was to lose one's birthright, nor did they assume that wage-earners and servants were synonymous categories (1972). Many writers would now accept that when the Levellers excluded 'servants' they meant only living-in servants and apprentices, not wage-earners with their own homes, and when they mentioned 'alms-takers' they intended that only those permanently in receipt of alms would be excluded from the vote. What is clear, however, is that Levellers set great store by independence, both economic and political, and that their interest lay in enabling a man to cast an *independent* vote. For this reason, they were prepared to stop short of the logical consequence of their belief in equal natural rights and to retreat from the position of universal manhood suffrage. Here the Levellers showed that they had not transcended traditional patriarchal assumptions about the role of male heads of household, and that their basic desire was to protect the small producer against the power of 'great men'. Their willingness to exclude beggars and servants, for example, could be reconciled with their more radical claims by maintaining that such men could be 'represented in the votes of their masters', and by recognizing Ireton's claim at Putney that those 'who depended on the will of other men' might be incapable of exercising the vote in their own right. To enfranchise dependent men might in these circumstances do more to entrench the power of great men than to restrict it. Such a policy would not enable the small craftsman, artisan, trader or farmer to challenge the power of oligarchy in politics and ensure the election of a representative body responsive to the interests and wishes of the 'middle sort of people' (Manning, 1976; Thompson, 1980).

The Levellers' constitutional and political proposals were detailed and wide-ranging, but they were not the only means by which the movement sought to advance the liberties of the people. Of great importance for the protection of the individual's rights in society were their plans for the reform of the law and the legal system. Full equality before the law, Levellers believed, was the chief protection for the individual's right to life, liberty and property, and the main guarantee that his 'self-propriety' (as Overton called it) would not be invaded by others. The health of the nation depended on swift legal reform, Lilburne had argued in 1645, and 'the Reformation of Courts of Justice, is a worke of absolute necessitye, without which . . . you shall have no Peace' (*Englands Birth-Right Justified*, quoted in Aylmer, 1975, p. 60). As well as plans for the local election of justices of the peace and magistrates, calls were made for the simplification of legal procedure so that it might be cheaper and easier to understand. English should be used in legal proceedings, the Levellers demanded, instead of Latin and law French. The Levellers wanted every plain man to be able to defend his interests at law without the help of professional lawyers, whom Lilburne especially detested, likening them to locusts who swarmed over the land devouring and impoverishing it. Mindful of the leadership's personal experience at the hands of various tribunals, the Levellers demanded that every individual should be free from arbitrary arrest, from imprisonment without trial, and from interrogation which might incriminate him. No man was to have special privileges at law because of birth and

45

status. Great emphasis was laid on the role of the jury, an essential institution in Leveller thinking. The jury was the embodiment of the freeborn men of England, men of independent mind who would judge a situation by the light of reason and reject the corrupting influence of faction. The right to trial by jury became a reserved power; and in March 1649 Lilburne bitterly criticized the new regime because the erection of the High Court of Justice meant that 'that great and strong hold of our preservation, the way of tryal by 12 sworn men of the Neighbourhood is infringed' (*Englands New Chains Discovered*, quoted in Aylmer, 1975, p. 143). The Levellers also wanted the reform of specific laws. Here their most urgent demand was for a change in the laws of debt. This would help, above all, the small trader who was often caught between the burden of defaulting or non-existent customers and the demands of suppliers clamouring to be paid. His 'cash flow' problems could easily land him in gaol, where he had no hope of earning anything to recoup his losses or meet his debts.

The individual's rights at law were crucial. So too was his right to liberty of conscience and worship. The involvement of individual Levellers in the campaign for religious toleration both predated and post-dated the emergence of the Leveller movement; indeed, as we have seen, it was this very issue which had brought several of the leading figures in the movement together for the first time. During its life, the movement's appeal to the sectarian interest was vital to its success, and although many sectarians in the end parted company with and repudiated Leveller ideals for a secular state, many Leveller supporters continued to identify themselves with the cause of radical religion in the 1650s. By 1647, a demand for religious toleration and the abolition of compulsory tithes had been incorporated into the Leveller platform; some Levellers, including Lilburne, had also begun to demand a complete separation of church and state. In the Large (or comprehensive) Petition of March 1647 the Levellers, operating as a mass political movement for the first time, argued that the suppression of allegedly heretical opinions should be stopped lest 'the most necessary truths, and sincere professions thereof may be suppressed'. They also demanded that tithes be abolished and not replaced by any other form of compulsory state maintenance for the clergy. In the first Agreement of the People, of November 1647, religious toleration became a reserved power; thereafter it maintained its clear status as one of the fundamental laws which no mere statute law could infringe. Religious toleration also provided the issue over which the Levellers broke with the Grandees in the Whitehall Debates of December 1648. Cromwell and the officers professed to accept that the state had no power to coerce a man's conscience, but they wished to retain the power to restrict the practices of so-called idolatry or atheism (in effect Roman Catholicism and the 'lunatic fringe' of radical religion). The Levellers felt that even this power was an infringement of religious toleration. None the less, in both the first and second Agreements of the People some kind of state church and non-compulsory form of public worship was still envisaged: in 1647 they were prepared to grant a future parliament 'the publike way of instructing the Nation (so it be not compulsive)'. By the time of the third Agreement in 1649 the Levellers had refined their position: they demanded a complete separation of church and state with no established church, no tithes and no other form of state maintenance for ministers. However, they now recognized a distinction between liberty of conscience and worship, on the one hand, and civil equality on the other. In this way Catholics were to be allowed to worship freely but could not hold public office. In its advocacy of such a broad degree of religious toleration – truly limitless for some Levellers, and including Jews and Muslims as well as Catholics – the movement was shown at its most egalitarian and humanitarian.

In the area of social and economic reform, the Levellers were less united and more ambiguous in their public pronouncements. Specific proposals for schemes of social welfare and for penal reform were popular among some sections of the movement, but they tended to be elaborated more in the writings of individuals than as an integrated part of collaborative policy documents. In 'Certain Articles' appended to an *Appeale from the Degenerate Representative Body* (1647), for example, Richard Overton argued the case for establishing schools and hospitals for the poor. The economic issues which figured in the Leveller programme tended to be those which particularly affected the urban middling sort. Overall, Levellers assumed that the system of private property would be retained, and officially they were quick to repudiate the notion that they were in the strict sense 'economic Levellers'. In the second and third Agreements, the powers reserved to the people were extended to include this very subject: the future Representative was expressly forbidden to 'levell mens Estates, destroy Propriety, or make all things common' (Wolfe, 1944, p. 301; Aylmer, 1975, p. 167). Here again, the Levellers were shown to be more concerned with the destruction of monopoly than the creation of equality. Mirroring faithfully the grievances of their 'middling' supporters, especially in London, they were content to press for the abolition of those privileged groups like the Merchant Adventurers who had caused so much hardship to the 'industrious people' in the nation, including tradesmen and seafarers. More radically, they were also prepared on

47

occasion to advocate the destruction of enclosures, the return of common lands to the people, and the abolition of 'base' or copyhold tenures. This would have benefited the smaller tenant farmer in the countryside faced with exploitation by a grasping landlord. Economic burdens on the people were also to be relieved by the abolition of the excise tax and by replacing it with more equitable forms of direct taxation. Beyond this, it is clear that only some members of the movement were prepared to countenance more egalitarian economic measures. William Walwyn was certainly one of those who had consistently condemned economic inequality. *The Power of Love* in 1643 was a particularly compelling statement of his views, but when he wrote *A Manifestation* in May 1649 on behalf of the other Leveller leaders, he conceded that economic levelling could not be forced on people against their will.

On the whole the individualistic liberal ideology of the Leveller movement encouraged their belief that political reform, not economic or social reform, would be the fount from which all other blessings for the common people would flow. Just as they believed that the source of the people's suffering was intrinsically political (in the long term the Norman Conquest, in the short term the corruption of parliament), so they believed that the remedies for these ills lay essentially in the political sphere. The economic issues which concerned them were principally those which affected the middling sort, the people to whom all Levellers would have given the franchise. In truth their economic and political thinking was all of a piece. They were against the agglomeration of wealth in a few hands, just as they opposed the concentration of political power in a few hands; conversely, they came out against complete equality of wealth just as they retreated from universal manhood suffrage. As Brian Manning concludes, if the Levellers hated the exorbitantly rich they also feared the very poor. Theirs was the 'characteristic doctrine of men of an intermediate status in society', the 'industrious' people or the middling sort (Manning, 1976, p. 315).

The Strengths and Weaknesses of the Movement

In attempting to build up the strength of their movement and win support for their programme, the Levellers showed themselves to be shrewd publicists and propagandists. They were very soon able to whip up demonstrations of pro-Leveller feeling in the capital, establish links with aggrieved elements in the counties, and tap feelings of discontent in the army. The use of the press, the organization of petitions and demonstrations, the development of a party structure, and the skilful deployment of the charismatic appeal of its leaders, quickly built up the impression of a mass political movement, especially in London.

The Levellers contributed in no small measure to the vast outpouring of pamphlets, tracts, treatises and other forms of printed polemic which marked the intellectual and emotional ferment of the 1640s. Although many of their tracts tackled complex issues in considerable detail and often with elaborate citation of biblical and other references, the Levellers also took care to speak directly to the ordinary people in a pungent, witty and cogent manner. Their rhetoric 'intensified the strengths of common speech', and its form was influenced by sources as diverse as plain preaching and popular drama (Heinemann, 1978). Whether it was the witty, vituperative style of Richard Overton's *The Baiting of the Great Bull of Bashan* (July 1649) or the histrionic appeal of Lilburne's account of his trial in 1649, *The Trial of Lieut. Collonel John Lilburne*, the Levellers showed they could play to an audience (Erskine-Hill and Storey, 1983). From June 1648 until September 1649 Leveller ideas also found their way into *The Moderate*, a weekly newsbook run by Gilbert Mabbott which circulated in London and the provinces. Other newsbooks which briefly favoured the Leveller cause were the *Perfect Occurrences* of Henry Walker, and the short-lived *Mercurius Militaris* of John Harris, a former professional actor turned printer to the army radicals (Brailsford, 1976).

The drawing up and presentation of petitions to parliament was another tactic shrewdly employed by the Levellers to organize and mobilize public opinion. The circulation of petitions like the Large Petition of March 1647, the Earnest Petition of January 1648, and the Humble Petition of September 1648 (as well as others on single issues like the arrest and imprisonment of the party leaders), enabled the movement to reach out and embrace large sections of public opinion and provided an essential focus and rallying-point for Leveller supporters. These petitions were often publicized and circulated for signature through the gathered churches in London and the provinces. *The Moderate* also helped to make their existence known. The act of presenting a petition to parliament became an occasion for mass crowd demonstrations in the streets of London. Likewise the arrest and trial of prominent members and the funerals of leading supporters afforded opportunities for shows of strength as well as for consciousness-raising. The funeral of Colonal Thomas Rainsborough on 14 November 1648 was the scene of much emotional drama. Crowds of supporters, many of them women, turned out sporting sea-green colours, which henceforth became a badge of the movement. In April 1649, the funeral of Robert Lockyer, an army Leveller who had been shot for taking part in a mutiny, provoked similar outbursts. Something of a personality cult was indeed an important element in the appeal of the movement. The quality of its leadership, particularly the charismatic appeal of John Lilburne, helps to account for the swift rise in the party's fortunes and its ability to draw large crowds of sympathizers to witness its public acts. Lilburne was well-suited to the role of 'populist and martyr', and his battles with authority provided a focus of identity for ordinary people. The resilience of the leadership after arrest and imprisonment, and their refusal to be silenced, also provided their followers with a model for popular action (Greaves and Zaller, 1983).

Partly to control the organization of public opinion through petitions and demonstrations, a party structure had grown up in London, and to a more limited extent in parts of the Home Counties. The City was divided up into wards, each of which sent representatives to a committee of the parish; in addition, twelve commissioners or agents were elected to act as a central executive committee for the party. Party subscriptions were levied according to a member's means, to support the cost of Leveller publications and other activities, and two treasurers were appointed to look after the party coffers. Various City taverns acted as party meeting-places: the party headquarters was situated in the Whalebone Tavern, and other favoured haunts were the Saracen's Head in Friday Street and the Windmill Tavern.

One method which, on the whole, the Levellers did not espouse was the use of organized violence or armed rebellion. For most of its life the party stuck to its belief in the power of man to judge things by the light of reason and did not abandon its faith in rational argument. Few contemplated the violent overthrow of the regime by an armed citizenry, or even by the New Model Army. Of course, the Levellers sought to influence the army, and radical supporters in the rank and file provoked mutinies, notably at Ware in 1647 and Burford in 1649, but this did not amount to an overall plan for the armed take-over of the regime. A few 'physical force' Levellers did exist, such as Major White and Captain Bray, and one ex-soldier William Thompson advocated armed risings in 1649; but when the party machine did come out in favour of mass armed rebellion in *The Remonstrance of Many Thousands of the Free People of England* (September 1649), it was merely the last fling of a dying movement (Aylmer, 1975; Hill, 1975).

The shrewd manipulation of issues and the mobilization of public opinion allowed the Levellers to build up support among apprentices, journeymen, small traders, craftsmen and artisans, and among some sections of the rural middling orders. Membership of a separatist

50

congregation and, especially, residence in and around London, were factors which predisposed men towards Leveller ideas. For much of the party's history, a 'typical' Leveller might be a small craftsman, perhaps in the textile trade, who had contacts with a gathered church and lived in one of the poorer suburbs of the capital. Levellers claimed to be able to call on 10,000 supporters in the metropolis and could produce several thousand signatures for a petition in London fairly quickly. But outside this area, and outside the 'middling' social groups, support for the movement was probably much less firm. There were organized Leveller groups in Buckinghamshire, Hertfordshire and Kent, and sympathy for Leveller agitation was expressed in petitions which arrived from much farther afield including at various times Somerset, Yorkshire, Oxfordshire, Leicestershire, Berkshire and Wiltshire. The monster petition, *The Remonstrance of Many Thousands of the Free People of England*, claimed to have 98,064 signatures. In addition, Leveller views attracted considerable attention in the army.

However, it would be misleading to infer from this that England was full of committed party supporters. The superficial strength of the Leveller movement during its petitioning campaigns masked underlying weaknesses. Sympathy with the grievances to which the Levellers gave voice was greater than support for the solutions to those problems which the Levellers advocated. Not all those who shared the Levellers' hostility to the 'powers that be' were prepared to translate their antagonism into demands for radical change; and of those who were prepared to countenance a radical solution, not all agreed that it should be the Leveller one. This last point was crucial to the party's fortunes: the Leveller movement rose in part because it fed on, inspired and became part of a radical coalition of interests in London, in the army and in the counties; when deserted by and isolated from the other elements in this radical coalition, its weaknesses were exposed. The weaknesses were both organizational and ideological. Organizationally, the Levellers were too dependent on the gathered churches; they had not built up their own representative machinery among the rank and file of the army; and they had done little to mobilize the peasantry as opposed to the urban middling orders. Ideologically, their programme was too frightening to the rich, too neglectful of the poor, and too innovative in its assumptions to embrace all the godly 'middling sort'. A closer look at some key episodes in Leveller history will illustrate these points.

First, it is clear that in 1647 the Levellers failed to capture the lasting support of the 'honest radicals' in the counties, although for a time support for the army against parliament was a unifying issue.

The 'honest radicals' were the 'godly party' in the counties, the connection between honesty and godliness being universally assumed (Underdown, 1978). The rank and file of those radicals for a while espoused a 'proto-Leveller' or Leveller-inclined position. Between March and June 1647, 'honest radicals' petitioned in support of the army. The first 'Leveller' petition came from Buckinghamshire and Hertfordshire and was presented to parliament along with a request for the release of Lilburne and Overton, who were at that time in prison. Other petitions to Fairfax followed in June from Buckinghamshire, Hertfordshire, Essex, Norfolk and Suffolk, with Essex making explicit reference to the Norman Yoke and Hertfordshire calling for the abolition of tithes and the relief of copyholders from arbitrary fines. But these proto-Leveller documents revealed two major weaknesses from the Leveller point of view: they did not have the backing of the upper echelons of the godly party, the 'establishment' radicals who might hold power in the county committees which had grown up to administer parliament's war effort in the localities, and geographically their spread was very uneven. The Levellers' appeal clearly diminished the farther from London one went, and in Underdown's opinion Bristol was the only place any distance from London from which 'genuinely Leveller' petitions have survived from 1647 (1978, p. 198). Later in the year, when Levellers embarked on a countrywide campaign to collect signatures for the first Agreement of the People, they were unable to build up a truly national organization. Despite reports of proselytization as far away as Nottinghamshire and Rutland, only in places close to London like Dartford in Kent were Leveller cells established.

In September 1648 the Levellers had another opportunity to canvass a wide spectrum of the radical interest. Their Humble Petition of 11 September reputedly had 40,000 signatures and sparked off responses from the tin-miners of Cornwall, the grand jury of Somerset, some farmers in the north, citizens in Newcastle, Bristol, Hull and York and the counties of Yorkshire, Oxfordshire, Leicestershire, Berkshire and Wiltshire (Brailsford, 1976, p. 355). As has been indicated, these petitions demonstrated support for the Levellers in a negative rather than a positive sense: they were engendered by the fear that a personal treaty would be concluded with the King (the Newport negotiations were currently taking place) and that all the gains of the war would be lost. They were not necessarily motivated by a strong commitment to all the details of the Leveller programme (Tolmie, 1977). Once the problem of the King was disposed of, there was no guarantee that other radicals would subscribe to a Leveller future. As David Underdown has remarked, the events of late 1648 and early 1649 were to show 'how few of the honest party were committed Levellers' (1978, p. 203).

The loss of support among the leaders of the sectarian community was extremely serious for the Levellers. The Levellers' stand on religious toleration had been an important part of their appeal to other radical groups, but not all sectarians were prepared to go further along the road towards accepting the secular state as a 'legitimate sphere of moral action in its own right' (Tolmie, 1977, p. 144). They were not willing to make the full transition from Christian liberty and virtue to equal natural rights. As early as the autumn of 1647, although the movement had already gained the allegiance of many individual sectarians and much organizational help from some of the gathered churches in London (including Particular and General Baptists), the enemies of the Levellers in the 'generality of congregations' publicly declared themselves. *A Declaration by Congregational societies in and about the City of London* argued against the Levellers' alleged attempt to make all men 'equal in power'. It was supported by several pastors, like the Baptists William Kiffin and Hanserd Knollys whom Lilburne had counted among his associates. None the less, throughout 1648 Levellers and sectaries continued to make common cause. But by 1649 a great rift had opened up between the Levellers and the Baptist pastors. The latter had decided to come to terms with the new regime in return for toleration, and formally dissociated themselves from the Levellers in March. Meanwhile the presence of the army in London had allowed the Grandees to win access to the separatist churches and to gain the loyalty of many religious radicals. Thereafter, it was difficult for the Levellers, reeling from other blows, to assume the role of political spokesmen for the godly (Tolmie, 1977).

The attitude of the sectaries was also vital for the all-important question of Leveller strength in the New Model Army. On this topic the work of Mark Kishlansky has recently commanded much attention (1978, 1979a, 1979b). Kishlansky argues that at its formation the New Model Army was not inherently radical. Its entry into politics and its espousal of radical causes in and after 1647 arose from its own material grievances, and from the desire to vindicate its own honour *vis-à-vis* parliament, not principally because of Leveller agitation and influence. Although by the beginning of the summer of 1647 the concerns of the army and of the Levellers were strikingly similar, Kishlansky maintains that the two movements had not yet made common cause. This probably did not reflect any reluctance on the Levellers' part. On 18 April a pamphlet entitled *A New Found Stratagem*, probably written by Richard Overton, had called on the army to rescue the people 'from sudden vassalage and slavery'.

Around the same time contacts were made between individuals in the army and Levellers in London. Edward Sexby, a trooper in Lord General Fairfax's regiment of horse, had already been in touch with Lilburne, and other soldiers who were to become the elected agents or Agitators of their regiments had Leveller connections. By June, the Levellers had increased their pleas to the army and by late July, Kishlansky surmises, Leveller ideas were beginning to have some impact on the soldiery. This is not to say, however, that when the General Council of the Army met during the summer the Levellers were really pulling the strings, or even that all Agitators were necessarily Levellers. The Levellers may have lent to army radicals a certain brand of political rhetoric, but their capacity to infiltrate and organize the rank and file was much more limited.

In September and October, however, the Levellers made a further effort. New Agitators were elected who were closer to the Leveller cause, and they agreed to recommend to the rank and file that the Leveller-inspired *The Case of the Armie Truly Stated* be accepted as a true statement of the army's grievances. *The Case* was redrafted in shortened form as an Agreement of the People, and it was this document which was then debated in the General Council of the Army at Putney between Grandees, Agitators and specially invited Leveller spokesmen. At first glance, the Putney Debates may seem to mark the high-water mark of Leveller influence, with the Grandees forced on to the defensive, their arguments subjected to close scrutiny by the radicals, and a high-ranking officer, Colonel Thomas Rainsborough, lending his passionate advocacy to the Leveller cause. Yet the Levellers lost at least some of the argument at Putney, and most of the action afterwards. They were outwitted at various points by Henry Ireton's intellectual skill (Tuck, 1979), and forced to concede ground on the franchise. Afterwards, their attempts to adopt direct action failed miserably and their inability seriously to disrupt army discipline was revealed. A small mutiny at Corkbush Field near Ware in Hertfordshire on 15 November was easily suppressed, and the Grandees reasserted their control over the army. The Grandees were helped in this by a split between the Levellers and the sectarian interest in the army, which mirrored the growing estrangement between the two movements in London. At Ware sectarian officers, especially the Particular Baptists, supported the Grandees and continued to do so throughout 1648 and 1649 wherever Leveller agitation threatened. Leveller ideas in general did not lose their impact among the rank and file, but, as we have seen, organizationally the Levellers were seriously weak. They had relied too much on the efforts of sectarians to organize the lower ranks (it was they who were behind the election of the first Agitators), instead of building up their own network; therefore when Leveller and sectarian interests diverged, the Levellers were denied this support and were unable to build up an organization of their own (Tolmie, 1977).

The suppression of the Ware mutiny may have marked the end of a chapter in the history of the army Levellers, but it did not entirely destroy their influence. In November 1648, when attempts to reach a settlement with Charles I had come to naught, Cromwell and Ireton again made overtures to Lilburne, but, as we have seen, despite the closeness of the two sides on some issues, the negotiations on a new joint Agreement of the People foundered on the question of religious toleration. The Levellers' next chance came when unrest in the army once again opened up the possibility of direct action. Mutinies were started in April–May 1649, the first of them in London resulting in the execution of Robert Lockyer. In May further mutinies which had started at Banbury (involving 1,000–2,000 men) and at Salisbury (involving two regiments) failed to make contact with each other. The Salisbury men tried to make their way along the Thames valley but were defeated at Burford. Thereafter, civilian Levellers still continued their agitation in London, but in truth the heart had gone out of the movement. Its best and perhaps only chance of gaining political power, support from the army, had completely disappeared. The protests over Lilburne's trial in London in 1653 could not revive these chances, and in 1659 when the collapse of the Republic was imminent, those Levellers who were still active (Lilburne had died in 1657) adopted a position very similar to the Harringtonian republicans. The Leveller programme as a whole was not relaunched: although religious toleration and equality before the law were still demanded, the franchise issue was dropped, and Levellers now put greatest stress on respect for law and order, the sanctity of property rights and on hostility to arbitrary rule (Hill, 1984).

In their heyday, then, it is clear that the Levellers exhibited great flair in exciting the popular imagination and dramatizing public events, but ideologically and organizationally their movement was severely flawed. The Levellers alienated key groups above them in the political and social structure (the ruling classes generally, the Grandees of the army, and the establishment radicals of the 'honest party'). They failed to consolidate their appeal to the middling orders whose interests they especially represented (they could not hold on to the allegiance of the godly party, and they did not capitalize on the grievances of the middling peasants). They also neglected or were actively hostile to those below them in the social scale (those without property were to be excluded from the franchise and social and economic reforms were limited). The Levellers both went too far and not far enough in their espousal of a new political and social order: in the end, their ideological and organizational base proved too narrow to achieve political success.

The historical significance of the Levellers must, however, be recognized. It is true that far from envisaging a completely democratic or egalitarian paradise, they were anxious to retain property, patriarchy and hierarchy. Their creed was that of liberalism and individualism, not socialism or equality. They wished to make the world safe for the people of the middling order, whose economic and political independence was their prime goal. Their economic and social vision was in some ways reactionary rather than progressive: they wanted to protect a vanishing world of small independent proprietors and traders, rather than look forward to the burgeoning of the middle class in a capitalist society. Their ideal of small communities and of a glorious Anglo-Saxon past were also symptoms of emotional nostalgia.

Nevertheless, they made significant ideological advances. Unlike other parliamentarians and republicans who were also wrestling with questions of sovereignty and trust, the Levellers developed their doctrines of popular sovereignty and trusteeship into a claim for the broad extension of active political rights. They went far beyond the doctrine of parliamentary sovereignty to place real and continuing power in the hands of the 'people', if not the 'poor'. Their stress on decentralization, and the individualistic emphasis of many of their social, economic and legal proposals, were deeply threatening to the ongoing concentration of wealth, status and power in the hands of a small elite. To support their programme, the Levellers advanced a radical theory of natural rights which looked forward to the later eighteenth century. Their political ideology was also notable for its rationalist and secularist aspects. Their appeal to reason was innovative, for although they combined this with a vision of the past as the locus of lost rights, they did not have the same view of history-as-precedent or of the sanctity of tradition as their more conservative contemporaries. Finally, although they made heavy use of religious arguments and sanctions for their views, their anticlericalism, their desire to separate church and state and to treat saints and sinners alike as equal citizens gave political theory 'a push . . . in the direction of avowed secularism' (Frank, 1955, p. 246). In sum, the Levellers' contribution to the political and religious ferment of the 1640s was immense.

4 The Religious Radicals

The challenge to the established order in mid-seventeenth-century England was not confined to those who devised new theories of the origins of government, or to those who advanced plans for the reshaping of the political order. The 1640s and 1650s also witnessed a proliferation of radical religious groups whose immediate concern was to attack the notion of a disciplined, established national church. These radicals included Particular and General Baptists, Quakers, Ranters, Seekers, Muggletonians and Fifth Monarchists, as well as members of separatist churches with no specific name. Some contemporaries would also have included the Independents with the sects because they adhered to the idea of the 'gathered church', but with the exception of a radical wing the Independents insisted that, church membership apart, they believed and worshipped very much as the Presbyterians did.

In a negative sense the religious radicals had much in common: they were opposed to the notion of enforced religious uniformity within one national church, territorially organized and universal in membership; they wished to extend liberty of conscience and worship; and they wanted to end the system of compulsory tithes. As such, they were united in condemning the theory and practice of the Anglican Church before 1642, and also the system of presbyterian church government which parliament erected in its place. However, beyond this desire for greater religious toleration and freedom of worship there was room for considerable diversity among the radicals. They differed, for example, on how complete the separation between the church and the state should be, and on what role (if any) was to be left to the civil magistrate in spiritual matters; they reached no exact consensus on whether to tolerate certain blasphemous or heretical opinions and certain politically suspect groups such as Catholics; and there were differences of opinion on what form of maintenance ministers should be afforded once tithes were abolished. In the 1650s, most religious radicals stood to gain from the looser, more tolerant and more liberal framework which Oliver Cromwell set up, but the retention of tithes and the setting up of boards of 'triers' and 'ejectors' to judge the fitness of candidates for, and incumbents in, parochial livings still aroused great hostility. Some radicals collaborated with the new arrangements for a loose 'national church', but most continued to press for greater freedom and the end to all forms of state maintenance for the clergy.

Across the radical spectrum there was also great diversity in theological opinion, in the degree of formal organization and internal unity which different groups demanded of their members, and in the political, social, economic and moral conclusions which the radicals drew from their religious beliefs. Some radicals, for example, such as Baptists and radical Independents, came together in recognizable 'churches' which had a formal structure; others like Ranters and Muggletonians were so loose and informal in their organization that one instinctively calls them 'groups', rather than 'churches'. Flexibility and fluidity were among the essential characteristics of many religious groupings, and the boundaries between them are hard to define: the gathered churches were not like present-day denominations which strive to maintain their distinctiveness in doctrine and organization. The dividing lines between different groups were often so confused that individuals could, and did, step over them easily and, indeed, numerous outstanding radical figures of this period made many transitions from one sect to another. This was in part a measure of the great variety of religious experiences on offer and the great spiritual excitement of those times, which encouraged men and women to abandon traditional restraints and seek out new forms of worship and belief. One such figure was Laurence Clarkson, a brilliantly 'made-to-measure' example of the ideological flux of the English Revolution (Morton, 1970, p. 115). Clarkson was brought up in the pre-war Anglican church and then progressed through Presbyterianism to become successively an Independent, a Baptist, a Seeker, a Ranter and, finally, a Muggletonian. Abiezer Coppe, a fellow-Ranter, had also been both a Presbyterian and a Baptist. John Milton, likewise, moved away from orthodox Calvinism to develop a highly personal and individual set of near-heretical beliefs, while John Lilburne, the separatist and Leveller, ended his life as a Quaker.

Origins, Influences and Assumptions

Without the conflicts and controversies of mid-seventeenth-century England and the breakdown of the old order in church and state, it is impossible to imagine such a flowering of radical religious beliefs. Yet it had its precursors in pre-Civil War England. At least as far back as Elizabethan times, radical dissent had had a shadowy underground existence in areas such as the Weald of Kent, parts of Essex and Cambridgeshire, the Chiltern Hills and parts of the West Riding of Yorkshire. Familist and Grindletonian groups had made their appearance, and their heterodox ideas were similar to some of those aired in the 1650s (Hill, 1978a). The Elizabethan Barrowists and Brownists had enunciated the principle of separation of church and state, and separatist churches had been formed whose members' inner religious life was close to the mainstream of Puritan practical piety. After the Elizabethan persecution, the existence of separate churches is hard to prove, but before the Civil War they had certainly been formed in London and Bristol, and probably also in Cambridgeshire and Wales. In the 1620s there were at least five General Baptist congregations in England, but their membership numbered perhaps only about 150 in total. By far the most important centre of radical activity was London, where from at least 1616 the church of Henry Jacob had spawned separatist offspring; yet on the eve of the Civil War only about 1,000 people attended the small group of separatist churches there (Tolmie, 1977). But as the political crisis between King and parliament deepened, so radical opinions began to surface. Lay preaching in London caught the public's attention, and separatists were crucially involved in popular demonstrations in the capital in 1641–2. Throughout the country, hostility to the payment of tithes found expression in riots and disturbances, and the question of lay – even popular – participation in the church at national and local level began to be discussed (Manning, 1976, 1978).

After 1642, the breakdown of the old order in church and state and the expression of radical opinion became mutually reinforcing. The inability of the parliamentarians to agree on what should replace the Laudian Anglican church opened the way for a proliferation of ideas on doctrine and church government. The relaxation of censorship allowed the radicals an outlet for their ideas, while social and economic dislocation provided a further stimulus to men to rethink their world. In this period it is impossible to separate political from religious thinking: the circumstances which promoted the rise of the Leveller movement also encouraged the emergence of religious radicalism (see chapter 3). Moreover, just as hostility to an established church and the desire for religious toleration drove many men to espouse radical politics, so too the failure of direct political activity or disillusionment with overtly political solutions may have driven them back to a reliance on specifically religious change. It must also be remembered that some radical demands, especially that for toleration, were the product of expediency as well as of principle.

Once the proliferation of opinions and the splintering of groups had taken place, toleration was the only way for minorities to ensure their own survival; but once a measure of toleration had been conceded, then this in turn ensured the perpetuation of dissent. Thus in the 1650s the increase in the number of radical groups was not merely the cause, it was also the consequence, of the regime's initial concession to radical demands.

The relationship between the religious radicals of the 1640s and 1650s and the Puritan movement is difficult to determine. Since the sixteenth century, Puritanism *as an ideology* had contained radical, even revolutionary, elements within it which challenged traditional notions of how power should be exercised in church and state, but in the early seventeenth century this was not translated into an organized movement of opposition or resistance (Collinson, 1982; Lamont, 1969; Walzer, 1964, 1965). Yet Puritan beliefs played an important part in the parliamentarian cause after 1642. Such was the breadth and flexibility of Puritan teachings that they influenced resistance to the Crown in and after 1642, informed the decision to replace episcopacy with Presbyterianism in the mid-1640s, sustained the more liberal policy of toleration under the Commonwealth and Protectorate, and also influenced the more radical critics of the Cromwellian system. However, it would be wrong to see religious radicalism in the 1640s and 1650s as simply the logical 'left-wing' extension of the type of Puritanism that had attracted a large following before the war. Other streams flowed into it too; some radical beliefs looked back to pre-Reformation heresy; and radical dissent often flourished in areas which had been relatively untouched by conventional Puritan piety and where the Puritan tendency within the pre-war Anglican church had been weak. Yet the background to much radical religious thinking is undeniably formed by the loose cluster of beliefs, attitudes and assumptions which we call Puritanism. Not all religious radicals remained Puritan in any clearly definable sense, nor did the more extreme among them have anything more than the slightest of connections with the orthodox Puritan movement. But what many radicals did, in effect, if not in intention, was to exploit the ambiguities and contradictions of Calvinist theology and Puritan belief, and develop and extend them in different directions.

Many historians would insist that adherence to Calvinist predestinarian theology is an essential characteristic of Puritan belief, yet many radicals departed from this and chose instead to embrace doctrines of free grace and universal salvation. Predestinarian beliefs – that is, the notion that some men (the elect) are saved and pre-ordained by God to receive everlasting life while others (the reprobate) have been damned and condemned to everlasting death – were retained by Particular Baptists, Fifth Monarchists, Muggletonians and by very many radical Independents. But both the Muggletonians and the Fifth Monarchists gave this basic doctrine a distinctive twist. The Fifth Monarchists interpreted the doctrine in a highly elitist way, believing that only members of their own sect were the elect, or the 'saints', who had the right to destroy the kingdoms of this world and rule in readiness for the (imminent) Second Coming of Christ. Other radicals repudiated altogether the predestinarian distinction between the elect and the reprobate, and believed that anyone who opened his heart to God could receive God's saving grace. The notion of salvation through God's free grace was what distinguished the General Baptists from their predestinarian and hence 'Particular' brethren. Quakers believed that 'God woulde have all men to bee saved Marke all men' (Hill, Reay and Lamont, 1983, p. 28). The more extreme radicals like the Ranters espoused antinomianism, the belief that Christ's atonement on behalf of mankind was sufficient to save all, so that men and women lived on earth in a state of grace and were not subject to external laws or the dictates of a moral code. Not all antinomians, however, took this doctrine to the extreme that the Ranters did in using it to justify strongly libertarian social and moral behaviour (Smith, 1983, pp. 8–9).

Attitudes to the question of salvation were closely linked to beliefs about the Spirit of God and its working within men. Conventional Puritans had emphasized the individual's direct relationship with God and had avowed that the Holy Spirit was in personal communion with the believer, but they had stressed the closest conjunction between Spirit and Word (that is, the Bible). The mainstream position was to believe that the Spirit spoke to man in, by or through the Word (or Scriptures). This was designed to uphold Scriptural authority and restrain purely individualistic interpretations, or spiritual fancies. Radicals, however, upset this equilibrium by putting their emphasis on the Spirit, stressing as the Quakers did that it dwelt within man, or even more extremely, that it dwelt in all creation (Nuttall, 1946). This most extreme interpretation of the doctrine of the Holy Spirit, which nearly all moderate radicals shied away from, led to charges that groups like the Ranters believed that 'the essence of God was as much in the Ivie leaf as in the most glorious Angel' (quoted in Morton, 1970, p. 73). It certainly led Gerrard Winstanley to assert that 'because God is to be known here and now within each one of us, worship of anything external must be idolatry or devil worship' (Hill, 1978b). The elevation of the authority of the Spirit against that of the Scriptures led to a variety of approaches to biblical interpretation. Some radicals remained directly inspired by what they regarded as the Bible's divine revelations, but stressed the role of the Spirit in guiding their interpretations and used the latter in a highly selective way; others (including the Independent John Owen) were interested in what we would regard as rigorous textual criticism; while the most extreme group began to highlight the mythical or allegorical nature of Bible stories and use them merely to illustrate arguments arrived at by other means. But only a tiny minority of radicals would have accepted William Walwyn's alleged statement that 'the Scriptures is so plainly and directly contradictory to itself' that he did not believe it to be the Word of God (Hill, 1975). Likewise, not all radicals by any means accepted the extreme implications of their beliefs by stressing the humanity of God, denying the Trinity or doubting that heaven and hell were geographical locations, as their more free-thinking brethren did.

Most radicals, however, responded in some way to the millenarian impulse which was also a part of Puritanism. Many historians now accept William Lamont's argument that in the early seventeenth century, some brand of millenarianism – the belief in the imminence of that period of 1,000 years when, according to the book of the Revelation, a messianic kingdom will be established on earth – was integral to the character of Puritanism, and indeed to the whole of English Protestantism (1969). For the Civil War period, an analysis of the works published by the most prolific Presbyterian and Independent divines between 1640 and 1653 has shown a millenarian strain in about seventy per cent of them (Capp, 1972). Millenarian hopes were encouraged by Puritan preachers in the 1640s as a stimulus to action for the parliamentarian cause, and the role of the common people in the 'last days' of the war against Antichrist was often stressed. Encouraged by the evident victories of the people of God during the Civil War, and anticipating great alterations in the order of things with the advent of the Republic, many religious radicals, not surprisingly, began to feel that the millennium was almost upon them. This intensified their spiritual excitement and justified, in the eyes of some, all manner of extravagant behaviour. Only the Fifth Monarchists, however, who drew much of their strength from the more millenarian-minded among the Baptists and Independents, translated their beliefs into an organized political movement, and perhaps only a minority of these were prepared to undertake revolutionary activity, in order to destroy the institutions of the old world in preparation for the Second Coming of Christ (Capp, 1972). As the 1650s progressed and the Second Coming failed to materialize, many radicals abandoned a specific and immediate sense of the millennium, but the general belief maintained the link between radicalism and earlier Puritanism.

One strain in the development of religious radicalism, therefore, was a tendency to extend and perhaps distort the libertarian and individualistic emphases in Puritanism. There were, of course, many other strands, including the highly elitist and even authoritarian elements in Fifth Monarchism. But a quest for liberty rather than discipline, and a search for freedom and toleration rather than unity and uniformity, were strong characteristics in much religious radicalism. They were demonstrated in both the internal arrangements of the gathered churches, and in the radicals' attitude to secular reform and relations with the political authorities.

The Gathered Churches and their Members

All radicals rejected the belief that church and state should be coterminous, and argued instead that individual churches should be formed on the basis of voluntary association, by the gathering together of the godly. Each congregation should be autonomous, and there should be no hierarchy of church courts as in the Anglican or Presbyterian system. The mere act of 'gathering' a church or congregation in this way was what defined many separatists, who in other respects do not fit easily into the groups we label 'Baptist', 'Quaker', etc. The more extreme and libertarian a radical group was in its beliefs, the less likely it was to establish a settled, formal congregation based on a church covenant, as the Independents did, or to erect regional networks of autonomous gathered churches like the Particular Baptists. In the case of the Ranters, Seekers, Muggletonians and some of the early Quakers, there was little formal organization to their religious meetings and no recognizably structured 'church' in the conventional sense. In some cases, the casual meeting of a few friends, perhaps even in a tavern, to express the workings of the inner spirit could count as a form of worship, though there might be no formal preaching, praying or even reading from the Scriptures. But this kind of informality was to be found only among the most radical.

At first, even the more moderate gathered churches allowed considerable latitude to their members to differ on points of doctrine, being more concerned to provide mutual fellowship and spiritual support than to maintain doctrinal uniformity. A separatist church was founded/at Bedford in 1650 explicitly on the principle of 'faith in Christ and holiness of life without respect to this or that circumstance or opinion in outward and circumstantial things ...' (quoted in Cross, 1972, p. 116). But increasingly many churches were forced to apply rules and standards to maintain the cohesiveness of the group and prevent disruption. In theory, congregational discipline was both collective and democratic and was exercised by the group over its own members on matters of belief and outward behaviour. The latter was an important source of concern to those more moderate churches who wished to protect themselves against accusations of condoning wild Ranter-like excesses. Increasingly, excommunication was used by some groups as a disciplinary weapon. Even the Muggletonians resorted to it: Laurence Clarkson was excommunicated in 1660 when he tried to challenge Lodowick Muggleton's leadership (Hill, Reay and Lamont, 1983).

The radicals' beliefs about the importance of voluntary association and their repudiation of compulsory tithes influenced their views on the relationship between the congregation and its minister. In general, most religious radicals wished to diminish the distance between pastor and congregation and were in some senses anticlerical. But whereas some groups (for example, the radical Independents) would accept the services of a professional ordained ministry, others repudiated the notion of the clergy as a separate caste altogether. In London by 1642 there were already probably eight or nine separate churches whose distinctive characteristic was that they had a lay pastor (Tolmie, 1977). The more ardent radicals displayed a virulent anticlericalism which both reflected and reinforced the support they received from the lower classes. Their hostility extended even to the Independent clergy, whom William Walwyn asserted 'pray, preach, and do all for money; and without it they do nothing' (Hill, 1975, p. 102). It was a commonplace among such radicals that, as William Erbery declared, the clergy were among 'the chiefest oppressors in the land' and that the payment of tithes was a means of depriving poor men of the just fruits of their labours. John Spittlehouse, a Fifth Monarchist, described ministers as 'very fountains of atheism and antichristianism', while Gerrard Winstanley launched his matchless invective against the clergy. 'Priests', he declared,

> lay claim to heaven after they are dead, and yet they require their heaven in this world too, and grumble mightily against the people that will not give them a large temporal mainten-ance. And yet they tell the poor people that they must be content with their poverty, and they shall have their heaven hereafter. But why may not we have our heaven here (that is, a comfortable livelihood in the earth) and heaven hereafter too, as well as you? (quoted in Hill, 1975, pp. 104, 140–1)

Hostility to tithes and to the ordained, university-trained clergy meant that radicals were prepared to welcome 'mechanic' preachers, gifted laymen from the middling and lower orders who were uneducated in the formal sense, but were admired for their spiritual worth. Far from receiving official state maintenance, such men were often sustained by the fruits of their own labours, or at most by the voluntary contributions of the congregation. In this way, the gulf between the preacher and the congregation was narrowed and the preacher became more responsive to the wishes of the people. Popular participation in worship was also encouraged, perhaps only in the form of discussion after a sermon, or more centrally in the act of worship as in the case of Quaker meetings. The radicals were also prepared to accept the consequences of their belief in the spiritual equality of the sexes by enhancing the role of women in the life of the gathered church. Many separatist congregations allowed women full rights in church government, to debate and to vote, but only the most radical (including some Baptists) allowed women to preach. Women achieved prominence in some of the London churches and among the Quakers, but women preachers have also been traced in places as far apart as Kent, Lincolnshire, Ely, Salisbury, Hertfordshire, Yorkshire and Somerset (K. Thomas, 1958).

The gathered churches, in the rationale behind their association, in their criteria for membership and in their internal power structure and organization, posed an implicit challenge to many contemporary social and political assumptions. The mere claim to the right to withdraw into the gathered church and to associate principally with one's chosen fellows could be seen as dangerously close to a repudiation of the authority of the state and of conventional social loyalties. As many Puritans had done before them, the radicals put adherence to the sect or the group above ties of kinship, family, neighbourhood or social deference. The 'horizontal' collective discipline of the congregation could undermine the 'vertical' hierarchical notions of command and obedience in society as a whole. The radical view of the ministry also challenged the value and purpose of education (most radicals were, not unreasonably, very suspicious of universities and 'book-learning'), while the importance attached to the 'mechanic' preacher questioned traditional assumptions about the qualities needed to exercise authority and leadership. The enhanced role of women could also be seen as deeply threatening to a patriarchal society. As a result, anxious contemporaries (not just the disgruntled Anglicans and Presbyterians, but supporters of the Republic too) were quick to read much social significance into symbolic acts like the Quakers' refusal to doff their hats to their superiors and their insistence on using the familiar 'Thee' and 'Thou' no matter whom they addressed.

As we shall see below, the radicals' threat to the established political and social order was much exaggerated by conservatives.

But their norms and values did prove attractive to elements within the middling and lower orders, who preferred to exchange their experience of traditional patterns of ecclesiastical and social discipline for the mixture of excitement and security offered by the sects. The appeal of some brands of radicalism to the lower orders was especially worrying to contemporaries, who were almost certainly led into overestimating their numbers by the public demonstrations of the more volatile radicals. A recent estimate by the historian John Morrill suggests that probably 'at no point in the critical period 1643–54 did more than five per cent attend religious assemblies other than those associated with their parish churches', although this figure probably rose after the emergence of the Quakers in the mid-1650s (1982, pp. 90 and 231). Some forms of congregational piety closely akin to those of the separatists were possible without a complete break from the parochial organization, but, even so, Morrill's estimates suggest that only a small minority of the population were at any one time committed to the practices of the radical separatists. Even the most sympathetic historians would not accept contemporary claims for the strength of the radicals. Quakers may have numbered at most tens of thousands, Baptists several thousands, grouped in about two hundred Particular and General congregations by the time of the Restoration, but Muggletonians and Ranters were perhaps never more than a few hundred in number, despite a contemporary claim that three thousand people were converted to Ranterism on a single occasion. Even the charge that sectaries and separatists were drawn from the lower classes has to be examined with care, for although the radicals undoubtedly lacked the degree of upper-class lay patronage which pre-war Puritanism had enjoyed, their attraction for other social groups was not always out of proportion to the latter's distribution in the population as a whole.

In geographical terms, the influence of some form of religious radicalism was felt in most parts of the country, but areas where new patterns of social organization flourished or where the traditional hierarchical chains of deference were weak may have been especially conducive to the growth of dissent. Thus some radical groups flourished in the so-called 'dark corners of the land', especially the north and west, and in other fen, moor and woodland areas where seigneurial and manorial control was weak and where orthodox Puritanism had not taken hold. Many groups also found ready support in towns, above all in London, where by 1646 there were already about three dozen separate churches in existence, with several thousand adherents (Hill, 1975; Hill, Reay and Lamont, 1983; Morton, 1970; Tolmie, 1977). Thanks to several excellent modern studies of religious radicals, it is possible to examine these broad statements in more detail.

Fifth Monarchists have been the subject of a major study by Bernard Capp (1972). They were not a discrete denomination or group in themselves, but were rather the political expression of a certain kind of millenarianism which drew heavily on extant Baptist and Independent congregations, among other sources of support. Described by Capp as an 'essentially urban movement' with a large number of members based in London, the Fifth Monarchists never numbered more than 10,000, probably less. In 1655, one of their leaders, Christopher Feake claimed 40,000 adherents and others claimed that 20,000 armed supporters could be raised in Wales alone, but this was unjustified optimism. The movement was to be found largely in the southern half of England (not in the 'dark corners' of the north and west), including Norfolk, Suffolk, Devon and Cornwall. In north Wales, the charismatic appeal of Vavasor Powell and Morgan Llwyd attracted a wide following. By contrast, most parts of the north of England, south Wales, many parts of the Midlands and the traditionally Puritan county of Essex proved uncongenial soil for the growth of Fifth Monarchism. Fifth Monarchist churches were formed in such ports as Bristol, Dartmouth, Portsmouth, Newport, Lewes and Sandwich, as well as many important inland towns with good road and river communications. Capp points out, however, that 'the areas of Fifth Monarchist strength show few common characteristics.'

The social composition of the Fifth Monarchists was the subject of hostile comment from contemporaries, one of whom labelled the movement as 'the worst of men, the Scum and very froth of baseness'. Even Christopher Feake admitted on one occasion that they were 'a company of illiterate men, and silly women'. Yet Capp's analysis shows that there were three distinct elements in the movement: a number of army officers (some gentlemen, some not), a number of clergy (some with army connections) and, thirdly, more typical of the rank and file than the leadership, persons in 'mechanic' occupations, including labourers, servants, apprentices and journeymen. Cloth-workers were dominant, comprising perhaps one-third of the membership, whereas agricultural workers (the largest group in the population as a whole) provided only about one-seventh of Fifth Monarchists. Many members were employed in manufacturing goods (in the food, drink and textile industries) and a smaller number came from the retail trades. In general, many supporters were drawn from occupations with a high level of social and economic insecurity. For them, as for other radicals, membership of the gathered church may have assured them of salvation in the next world, filled their lives with a sense of much-needed excitement at the prospect of the approaching millennium; and provided comfort and companionship in the here-and-now.

In contrast to the urban base of the Fifth Monarchists and other radical groups, the Quakers were extremely successful in building up a rural following. In part, this was because they were in the vanguard of popular agitation against tithes; from 1654 onwards they became a haven for many who in the 1640s and early 1650s had been involved in anti-tithe activity (Reay, 1980a). They were able to harness existing feeling against tithes to their cause in Somerset, Kent, East Anglia, Lancashire, Cumberland, Bedfordshire, Huntingdonshire, Cambridgeshire and possibly Yorkshire. Other areas of support included Buckinghamshire and Gloucestershire. The Quaker movement became particularly associated with parts of the north and west, including the Lake District. In 1659 they were able to collect 15,000 signatures for a petition against tithes solely from the counties of Westmorland, Cumberland, Lancashire and Cheshire. Especially in the north, Quakerism may also have advanced in some communities because of the precedent set by older radical traditions, such as the Familist or Grindletonian, so that in its early days there may have been many kinds of Quakerism rather than one coherent movement (Hill, 1984). From its base in Westmorland and among the yeomanry of the West Riding of Yorkshire, Quakerism none the less launched a nationwide campaign which drew support away from other radical groups as it spread south. The social composition of the early Quakers shows that the movement appealed to fairly prosperous yeomen and traders, as well as to humbler husbandmen and artisans, with the upper ranks of the middling orders being in some areas very prominent. Some gentlemen, and some professional men, were also among the first converts. Perhaps only the very top (aristocracy) and the very bottom (paupers and landless labourers) of the social scale were under-represented in the early movement (Cole, 1957; Reay, 1980a, 1980b; Vann, 1969).

Muggletonians tended to be slightly more wealthy than the average citizen (Hill, Reay and Lamont, 1983). Their membership did include a number of (arguably eccentric) gentlemen and merchants, but it was principally drawn from shopkeepers and artisans. Although it is not always easy to isolate those who joined the movement after 1660 from those who joined before that date, it seems that the Muggletonians did not prove attractive to labourers or servants, and that a Muggletonian was more likely to be a retailer or an artisan than a wholesaler or a large producer. Literacy standards were relatively high in the group, which also indicates that its following came from among the middling orders. London was an important centre of Muggletonian activity, but groups were also formed in various parts of the Midlands, the south of England and in Ireland.

Ranters, like Muggletonians, are hard to identify, but their historian A.L. Morton claimed that, despite the paucity of numbers, their influence was felt throughout England (1970). Individual groups of Ranters may only have numbered about a dozen, but they had some strength in the poorer areas of London, among depressed artisans and labourers, while reports of Ranter activity came from Abingdon, Leicester, Coventry, York, King's Lynn, Uxbridge, Ilford, Winchester, Berkshire and Kent. In general terms, Ranterism seems to have attracted the support of wage-earners and small traders in towns rather than agricultural workers in the country.

Finally, General Baptists were particularly noticeable in the east Midlands and in Kent, while Particular Baptists – a much larger and altogether more structured and formal group than some of the extremists – had centres of strong affiliation in London, Berkshire, the Midlands and the western counties, as well as Wales and Ireland. The Particular Baptists, in fact, built up successful regional associations to support and lend succour to weaker churches, each of which had close relations with a group of London advisers (White, 1966).

Economic, social and environmental conditions, especially among the middle and lower orders, thus play a large part in explaining the composition and distribution of religious radicalism in the 1640s and 1950s. But an additional factor in the rise of many radical groupings was the influence of charismatic preachers and leaders. Just as the intellectual abilities and personal qualities of William Walwyn, Richard Overton and, above all, John Lilburne, were crucial to the success of the Leveller movement, so too the inspiration and appeal of individual religious leaders was central to the advance of the separatist or sectarian cause. The rise and fall of Baptist and Fifth Monarchist centres in Wales, for example, reflected the influence of charismatic preachers, whose departure from a certain area might spell the end of a gathered church, as quickly as their advent had signalled its rise. All movements, of course, have their leaders, but the stamp of some radical ideologues – and demagogues – on their followers was especially strong. The Muggletonians, for example, relied heavily on the inspiration of John Reave and Lodowick Muggleton, under whom each local area had its special leaders: James Whitehead in Essex, Christopher Hill in Kent, Dorothy Carter in Derbyshire, Colonel Robert Phayre in Ireland, among others. The Quakers' evangelical drive owed much to several outstanding figures including George Fox, Edward Burroughs and

James Nayler. Abiezer Coppe, Laurence Clarkson, Joseph Salmon and Joseph Bauthumley played a crucial role in articulating the tenets of the Ranters. Fifth Monarchism owed much to the talents of Thomas Harrison, John Rogers and Vavasor Powell, as well as to ministers like Christopher Feake and John Simpson. Indeed, the history of religious radicalism is littered with a host of exciting and adventurous characters whose personal eccentricities often rivalled their intellectual power, but whose contribution to the radical ferment was immense. William Erbery, William Sedgwick, John Saltmarsh, William Dell, Arise Evans, Richard Coppin, Samuel Fisher, John Warr and, towering above them all, Gerrard Winstanley, are crucial figures in the story of those who in their contemporaries' eyes tried to turn the world upside down. Yet ironically, as we shall see in the next section, the alarm which their ideas and activities created was greatly out of proportion to the real threat which they posed to the political and social stability of successive regimes.

The Radicals and the Secular World

Just as the principle of voluntary association in a gathered church implicitly subverted traditional notions of social loyalty and organization, so conservatives believed that other radical religious beliefs challenged existing institutions. The radical agitation against tithes and against lay impropriation was deemed to be particularly threatening, not merely because refusal to pay was a challenge to the existing law, but because it was also a threat to property rights. The fear that many radicals were economic levellers in disguise was increased when some groups, including Quakers and Fifth Monarchists, advocated the abolition of copyhold and customary tenures and 'feudal relics', and when often violent antagonism towards the rich was expressed by radicals like the Ranters. The belief that God dwelt in all men and in all creation lent itself readily to a denial of outward economic and social distinction, and Ranter writers expressed most forcefully the idea that God himself was the great Leveller who would arrive shortly to bring down the great ones of this world. The appeal to a primitive biblical communism by people like Abiezer Coppe, George Foster and Laurence Clarkson did not constitute a coherent plan for economic or political revolution by any means, but in the hands of conservatives such extravagant utterances could conveniently be used as a stick with which to beat all radicals, whatever their views.

Similarly, the remarkably uninhibited sexual behaviour of some radicals, which was justified by their belief that the moral law had no authority over those who lived in a state of grace, aroused both

70

opprobrium and ridicule which, like charges of economic levelling, was extended to cover many more than the guilty parties. Ranters in particular were noted for their sexual licence, and fear of the threat to social order which this implied was a strong motive behind the Rump's investigation into Ranter activities in 1650, and the subsequent passage of the Blasphemy Act. A persuasive tract published by John Reading in 1650 condemned the Ranters' self-indulgence. 'They affirm that all Women ought to be in common,' he wrote,

> and when they are assembled together (this is a known truth) they first entertaine one another, the men those of their own sex, and the Women their fellow females: with horrid oaths and execrations, then they fall to bowzing and drink deep healths (O cursed Caitiffes) to their brother God, and their Brother Devill; then being well heated with Liquor, each brother takes his she Other upon his knee, and the word (spoken in derision of the sacred Wit) being given, viz. *Increase and Multiply*, they fall to their lascivious imbraces, with a joynt motion &C. (quoted in Smith, 1983, p. 19)

Many radicals in the 1640s and 1650s were certainly very liberal in their attitudes to sexual and domestic relations. Milton was not alone in advocating divorce, and many would have defended the right of a godly woman to desert an ungodly husband. The Quakers, some Baptists and others, including Gerrard Winstanley, wanted to solemnize marriage by declaration before the congregation and abolish other types of civil and religious ceremony. Some radicals did deserve their reputation for sexual libertinism. Abiezer Coppe and Laurence Clarkson advocated complete sexual freedom, the latter arguing that to the pure all things are pure, and that freedom from the guilt of sin was only achieved by being free to sin. The instability of sexual relations within some radical groups no doubt reflected the itinerant life which many evangelical preachers and their followers led, but in contrast it must be stressed that many other radicals deliberately cultivated a life of asceticism.

The fear with which moderates and conservatives viewed the supposed threat from the religious radicals is not borne out by an examination of the impact of their activities on the political and social scene. We must remember first of all that many brands of religious radicalism were explicitly tolerated by the regimes of the 1650s. The Instrument of Government of December 1653 formally marked the extension of toleration to all 'such as profess faith in God by Jesus Christ . . . provided this liberty be not extended to Popery or Prelacy, nor to such as, under the profession of Christ, hold forth and practice licentiousness'. This definition was markedly tightened up in the Humble Petition and Advice of 1657, but still the degree of toleration granted under the republican regimes was considerable, the provisions of the Blasphemy Act notwithstanding. Also, the Cromwellian system of 'triers' and 'ejectors', which in theory should have been repudiated by all those who eschewed contact with parochial organization and compulsory tithes, in practice secured the collaboration of some radicals. At least 130 Independent ministers and some Baptists accepted parochial livings, while also serving their gathered church, and many others carried out non-parochial preaching or teaching appointments within the state church (Cross, 1972, p. 112). Moreover, although much radical agitation was implicitly political, in the sense that the religious system which it opposed was a system imposed and sustained by the state, overt political organization on the part of the radicals was not the norm.

The major exception to this was, of course, the Fifth Monarchist movement. Organized Fifth Monarchism dates from the end of 1651, and it played a significant political role until the founding of the Protectorate. For a time Fifth Monarchists had believed that the Rump Parliament would establish Christ's kingdom in England, but when confidence in the Rump waned after the battle of Worcester, Fifth Monarchism became an organized movement with the explicit aim of enabling the saints to seize power. However, when their chance came, after the dissolution of the Rump and the summoning of the Barebones assembly, only twelve Fifth Monarchists secured election. The defeat of the radicals by the more conservative members of Barebones' parliament and the setting up of the Protectorate drove the movement into opposition, although it was divided on the tactics to be pursued. Soon afterwards it lost the support of leading Baptists and Independents. The army still contained some leading Fifth Monarchist figures (including Major-General Harrison) who could call on many republican sympathizers among the officers, but arrests in the country and in the army, following the discovery of anti-protectoral plots, seriously weakened the movement. In 1657, an attempted rising in London led by Thomas Venner and backed by radical plebeian elements failed to attract sufficient support, and thereafter the strength of the movement was reduced even further. A brief resurgence in the troubled days of 1659 did little more than frighten conservatives and help to fuel the general belief that stability and settlement could best be achieved by the return of the King.

The Quakers also played a part in sectarian agitation in 1659. Since their inception, Quakers had clashed with the authorities over their opposition to tithes: at least 1,000 were proceeded against for non-payment between 1653 and 1659 (Reay, 1980a). As with other radical activity, this had served to alarm and alienate moderate opinion, especially among the propertied classes. In the 1650s the Quakers had not renounced political activism as they were to do later in the century, and throughout the decade they fearlessly testified against magistrates and parsons. In 1656 they became involved in the elections to the second Protectorate parliament. Quakers regarded the Protectorate as a betrayal of the 'Good Old Cause', but in general they did not become embroiled in plots, within the army or elsewhere (unlike the Fifth Monarchists and other republicans). In 1659, they were politically active once again and tried to reach an agreement with the restored Rump. This alarmed moderates, who complained that Quakers were being reintroduced as justices of the peace and militia commissioners and were being armed. But the Quakers were divided in their attitudes to the military *coup d'état* of October 1659, and while their own strength was not enough to shore up the restored Commonwealth, their alleged influence – like that of the Fifth Monarchists and other radicals – helped provoke the conservative backlash which led to the restoration of the monarchy (Cole, 1956).

The fate of the Quakers and Fifth Monarchists may suggest where the positive significance of the religious radicals lies: in the realm of ideas, not that of political events. In their religious and social thinking the radicals made major advances, but their political influence was in many ways the reverse of what they intended: instead of bolstering the 'Good Old Cause', in the short term they in fact aided the conservative reaction. In the longer term, however, the balance is different. The existence of dissent, and with it the *de facto* case for toleration, was to be an ineradicable legacy of the Interregnum.

5   The Diggers and the Clubmen: A Radical Contrast

Neither the Levellers nor the religious radicals had as their primary goal the setting up of a fully democratic and egalitarian society in the secular world. The Levellers had made great ideological advances towards a rationalist, secularist view of political power, but their programme was geared towards liberalism and individualism, not socialism, communism or democracy for all. The religious radicals had placed great emphasis on freedom and equality in spiritual matters, but they had not organized a political movement to translate their egalitarian ideas from the spiritual to the secular plane. We now turn to the ideas and influence of Gerrard Winstanley, who attempted the fusion between radical theology and rationalist political theory and who translated his spiritual beliefs into an economic and political vision of full equality and democracy; we will also look at the activities of the Digger movement, who sought to put Winstanley's ideas into practice by setting up communities based on the common ownership of land. The Digger movement was a response to a democratic call for radical action on the basis of a radical programme: a fitting conclusion perhaps for a study of radicalism in the English Revolution. But in order to stress how untypical such popular action was of the 'governed' as a whole, this book will end with a brief look at the Clubmen movements of the 1640s. This alternative brand of communitarian protest firmly suggests that popular activism in this period could most readily be launched in defence of conservative, rather than radical, views.

The Beliefs and Aims of Gerrard Winstanley

Gerrard Winstanley's views went through several stages of development, from 'chiliastic mysticism' to 'progressive rationalism' to 'practical communism' (Petegorsky, 1940). He evolved a system of thought which combined three main elements: a radical religious belief in God-as-reason and in God's immanence throughout all creation; an economic interpretation of equal natural rights; and an expanded version of the historical myth of the Norman Yoke which embraced economics and religion as well as law and politics. His especial insight was to see that state power depended on the property system (Hill, 1973). He believed that economic freedom must come before political freedom, and that an egalitarian economic and social order could be attained only by the collective action of the common people. The period from December 1648 to January 1649 was crucial in Winstanley's intellectual development: it was then that he was converted to communism and combined his theological with his economic beliefs. In this way he made the transition from a consideration of 'righteousness' to a striving for 'freedom'.

Few details of Gerrard Winstanley's early life are known. He was born in Wigan on 10 October 1609. His father was probably a textile dealer and the family had strong Puritan connections. In 1630 Winstanley came to London and was apprenticed in the cloth trade. In 1637 he was made a freeman of the Merchant Taylors' Company and set up as a cloth merchant. In those times of political uncertainty and economic depression his business did not prosper, and in 1643 he ceased trading and moved to Surrey. There he worked as a hired labourer herding cows until 1648. In that year he published several religious tracts couched in highly mystical and sometimes obscure language. His conversion to communism was intimated in *The New Law of Righteousness* (January 1649), and thereafter he wrote over a dozen political tracts, culminating in *The Law of Freedom in a Platform* (1652), which outlined his most elaborate plans for the foundation of a new society.

Winstanley believed that God is in every man and woman and in all creation; to worship anything external was therefore idolatry. In *The Saint's Paradise* (1648), he wrote:

> He that looks for a God without himself and worships God at a distance he worships he knows not what but is led away and deceived by the imaginations of his own heart . . . but he that looke for a God within himselfe and submits himselfe to the spirit of righteousness that shines within, this man knows whom he worships for he is made subject to and hath community with that spirit that made all flesh in every creature within the globe. (quoted in Petegorsky, 1940, p. 132)

For Winstanley, God was not a personal deity; rather he conceived of God as a principle which gave unity and harmony to the universe and enabled men to live peacefully with their fellows. He identified God and the Spirit with reason – the 'highest name that can be given' to God – and for him reason was the spirit of co-operation. Reason tells a man 'do as you wouldest be done unto' and 'is thy neighbour hungry and naked today, do then feed him and cloathe him, it may be thy case tomorrow and then he will be ready to help thee.' But Winstanley recognized that the devil or 'Serpent' – the spirit of selfishness, the opposite of reason – was also within man and he believed that men would become perfect only when they were taken up into the spirit of God within them and lived by the light of reason. He believed that all men would in the end be saved, and he envisaged a Second Coming which he described as 'the rising of Christ in sons and daughters'. By this he meant that the spirit of co-operation would one day be realized throughout mankind and a communistic society would be established on earth.

By January 1649, for reasons which remain obscure, Winstanley had translated his concern with the clash of spiritual forces within man into an analysis of the external social manifestations of that struggle. His spiritual arguments were increasingly clothed in political language. He now maintained that at one time men had lived in a state of harmony and common ownership of land, for 'in the beginning of time the great Creator, Reason, made the earth to be a Common Treasury, to preserve beasts, birds, fishes and man.' Then the spirit of covetousness and selfishness had arisen within man, together with the desire for private property. Once a few men had gathered property into their own hands, the rest had been forced to become wage labourers and had been alienated from the land. Following this, a political and legal system – the apparatus of 'kingly power' – had been erected to bolster the tyranny and protect the privileges of the few. The solution to the strife and misery which such a system created was to make the earth a common treasury again, so that social harmony might prevail and the preservation of all men be assured.

For Winstanley, common ownership of land, communism in production as well as in distribution, was the basis of individual freedom and social equality. He supported this argument with an appeal to natural law, which he believed gave to man free and collective access to the means of subsistence. 'True freedom lies where a man receives his nourishment and preservation, and that is in the use of the Earth', he wrote in 1652. In this way, Winstanley drew the economic consequence of the Leveller doctrine of equal natural rights. He also developed an economic reinterpretation of the Norman Yoke, for he believed that private property had been introduced into England by the Norman Conquest. By dividing up the land among his followers, William I had introduced the power of lords of the manor into England. Thereafter, he went on, English-men, who had been divorced from the land and forced to work as bondsmen, had been progressively enslaved by 'kingly power', which preserved the rights of all landlords as well as those of the monarch. The whole had been buttressed by a legal system which protected property and confounded the common people, and by a religious system whose corrupt clergy inculcated the duties of obedience and reinforced oppression by the imposition of tithes. As we have seen, Winstanley's anticlericalism was of the most virulent kind and was occasioned by his belief that the church had occupied a key role in the structure of monarchical oppression and landlord exploitation.

Winstanley believed that very little of this apparatus of 'kingly power' had been dismantled by the execution of the monarch in 1649 – only 'the top bow is lopped off the tree of Tyrannie' – and he maintained that the people had been ill-rewarded for their sufferings in the Civil War. He therefore called upon the common people to take direct action to assert their claim to the waste and common lands of England, as a first step towards the abolition of private property altogether. They were to 'lay the foundation of making the Earth a Common Treasury for all, both rich and poor'. He insisted, however, that those without property must act peacefully; they must not forcibly expropriate private property as such (that is, freehold land), but should merely occupy waste and common lands to which they had a traditional legal right. Winstanley was always vague about how the transition from the assertion of squatters' rights to the abolition of all private property could be effected. In part he seems to have believed that rational argument and practical example would prevail; but, more shrewdly, he also realized that if men ceased to offer their labour for hire and worked only in newly formed collectives, then landlords would be forced to give up private lands which they could not cultivate alone, and their property would gradually pass into common ownership.

Winstanley's call to action resulted in the setting up of ten Digger communities in 1649–50, but they were easily suppressed by the authorities (see below). This led Winstanley to rethink his methods but not to abandon his ideals. In 1652 he published *The Law of Freedom in a Platform* which showed a clearer recognition that the poor would need the help of those in power if they were to achieve their aims: the tract was dedicated, hopefully, to Oliver Cromwell. By this time, some of Winstanley's earlier buoyant optimism about a direct call to popular action had gone, and indeed no new Digger communities resulted from the publication of this major work. *The Law of Freedom* set out, in some detail, proposals for the institutional structure of Winstanley's ideal society, and addressed itself to problems of law, administration, parliament, religion and education. It enshrined a vision of a predominantly agrarian society, based on common ownership of land, with some men engaged in basic crafts. All productive resources were to be communally owned and wage labour was forbidden. Commerce (buying and selling) was, likewise, outlawed and was to be replaced by the exchange of goods according to need. Storehouses would be set up to collect and distribute the fruits of the earth and all manufactured goods. Money would be unnecessary and its use confined to foreign trade. The internal sale and purchase of land or goods was to be made a treasonable offence, punishable by death, and penalties were also laid down for anyone who refused to work.

Winstanley's political system allowed for a parliament, elected annually on the basis of universal manhood suffrage. In the long term its positive functions would be quite limited, but initially it was to play an important role in removing all obstacles to the unrestricted development of the ideal communal system. Its first task would be to make all common, waste, abbey, bishops' and Crown lands available to the poor for cultivation. All public officials were to be elected, again by universal manhood suffrage, and could hold office for only short periods to avoid the emergence of a professional bureaucratic class. For Winstanley, even more than for the Levellers, power was to be largely devolved to local communities. All parishes and boroughs were to elect officials to administer law, oversee production, supervise the storehouses and arrange for the education of the young. Local 'peacemakers' were to resolve conflicts and preserve harmony, and something like neighbourhood tribunals were envisaged. There were to be no professional lawyers, a caste whom Winstanley disliked almost as much as he hated the clergy. A locally based people's militia would replace a professional army. In Winstanley's utopia, all men were to enjoy complete freedom of religious belief and there was to be no institutionalized religion: no state church, no professional clergy, no tithes and no conventional sabbath observance. The weekly day of rest was to be given over to social intercourse and secular instruction. Men whom we might call 'ministers' were to be elected, but instead of preaching or administering the sacraments they were to give 'sermons' on matters of secular public interest, such as history, current affairs and the natural sciences. In the field of education, Winstanley's views were also very advanced. He believed that education should be both free and compulsory for all boys and girls and that it should emphasize practical training in useful crafts and skills. Like many other radicals, he abhorred the clergy's monopoly of higher education and distrusted book-learning. His plans had a strong utilitarian and scientific bent and were designed to promote and reward technical innovation.

Winstanley's beliefs and programme mark the peak of radical, innovative tendencies in the history of political, religious and social thinking in the 1640s and 1650s. But, as with others, his unique contribution to the development of a radical ideology was not matched by the impact of his beliefs on actual events. The Digger movement, to which his ideas gave rise, had a brief and insubstantial life; in strength and numbers it could not compare as a form of popular communal action with other associations of a more conservative hue.

The Digger Movement

At the beginning of 1649, when both economic misery and political excitement were widespread, Winstanley's belief in popular action had seemed to have a chance of winning some support. 'Action is the life of all', he had declared, 'and if thou dost not act thou dost nothing.' The first experiment in practical communism took place on Sunday 1 April 1649. A group of poor labourers led by Gerrard Winstanley and William Everard, a radical who had been dismissed from the army, gathered on St George's Hill in the parish of Walton-on-Thames in Surrey. They began to dig up the wasteland there, planting it with corn, parsnips, carrots and beans. These men at first called themselves 'True Levellers'. It is possible that they had a tenuous connection with a very radical group of Levellers in Buckinghamshire, who had published a plea for equality of property in December 1648 entitled *Light Shining in Buckinghamshire*; but the Leveller movement proper rushed to dissociate itself from these early communists. St George's Hill was close to the radical suburbs of south London, and in an area where enclosure had caused much hardship to poor people. But despite predictions that thousands would flock to the Digger standard, over the next few weeks only thirty or so joined the colony. Their leaders were summoned to appear before Fairfax, but overall the Diggers suffered more harassment from local landlords and freeholders than from the army. When they attempted to cut down timber, the local lord of the manor seized his opportunity to sue them for trespass. In August 1649, the original colony was driven off the land and moved to Cobham a few miles away. There, local people repeatedly tried to destroy their crops, assault them and tear down their shelters. About the same time, however, other communities were being formed in different areas. By the spring of 1650, there were settlements at Wellingborough in Northamptonshire, Cox Hall in Kent, Iver in Buckinghamshire, Barnet in Hertfordshire, Enfield in Middlesex, Dunstable in Bedfordshire, Bosworth in Leicestershire and at two other locations in Gloucestershire and Nottinghamshire (Hill, 1975). These Diggers cannot have numbered more than a few hundred in total, if that: the names of seventy-three are known from the Surrey colonies, together with a few more from other sites. By March 1650, the colony at Cobham had sent out agents to the Home Counties and the Midlands to drum up financial support, but their efforts were in vain. In April, the community at Cobham was finally suppressed, the other Digger experiments collapsed, and Gerrard Winstanley was left to contemplate the truth of his suspicion that 'Every one talks of freedom, but there are but few that act for freedom; and the actors for freedom are oppressed by the talkers and verbal professors of freedom' (*A Watchword to the City of London and the Army*, Hill, 1973, p. 129).

The Clubmen: A Postscript

The act of digging had been the ultimate expression of the fusion of radical ideas and radical action by the common people in the English Revolution. Yet the fate of that adventure had shown not merely the strength of established authority, but also the weakness of the attraction which new visions of society held for the lower classes. The Diggers' action had been a communistic protest. Ironically, it was another form of community action, but this time in support of a deeply conservative programme, which more convincingly displayed the potential of the 'governed' for direct action during the Civil War.

The strength of the Clubmen movements of the mid-1640s provides an instructive comparison with that of the Diggers, and indeed of the Levellers. The Clubmen have been described as 'radical conservatives', activist 'neutrals' in the context of the Civil War, who wished to protect traditional rights and values in church and state and to defend their local communities from external attack. The maintenance of law and order, the preservation of private property, and an adherence to the old Protestant religion, were their favourite themes. They arose in direct response to the experience of war. Their aim was to fend off the depredations of the opposing armies, protect the integrity of their counties in the face of the new administrative machinery which both royalists and parliamentarians had built up to sustain their war effort and, in general, to resist the encroachments of either side on their traditional communities. Although tactically the Clubmen might have to compromise and collaborate with one side or the other, and may have had more covert sympathy for one side than the other, they remained essentially bands of armed neutrals whose overriding desire was for peace (Morrill, 1976).

Clubmen ideology involved elements of thought similar to those espoused by Charles I's moderate parliamentarian critics in 1640–2. Clubmen had a legalistic caste of mind; they articulated the same conservative, localist assumptions; they appealed to similar ideas of known laws and ancient liberties; and they professed the same unrealistic belief that the two sides in the war were essentially compatible and could readily be made to work in harmony together to restore the balanced polity. They sought an accommodation at national level and a local truce in their own communities, and wished to restore the administration of justice and maintenance of order to the traditional organs of local government.

Each Clubmen association was in origin essentially a popular peasant movement. The initiative came from the rural middling orders, and yeomen and similar men of property formed the backbone of the movement. In most cases, leadership did pass into the hands of the gentry (although Somerset retained a healthy distrust of the elite). The rank and file none the less contained men of all social classes below the level of the aristocracy. The Clubmen emphasized in their propaganda horizontal rather than vertical ties of social loyalty, appealing to notions of 'neighbourliness', 'mutual trust' and fraternal association. The associations also afforded the middling orders some opportunity for independent organization, not directly dependent on orders from above. The Somerset Clubmen went further, outlining plans for the peasant community to assume the functions of the traditional authorities, to elect their own officers and raise levies in each parish to recompense any labourer who wished to join them for loss of earnings.

In 1645–6 Clubmen movements were to be found in most of the southern and western counties of England and in parts of the Midlands and Wales. Among the most famous are those in Wiltshire, Dorset, Berkshire, Sussex, Hampshire and Somerset. Most associations did not maintain permanent standing forces, but evolved mechanisms for summoning men to arms from village communities when danger from marauding armies threatened. The sheer weight of numbers which the Clubmen could command is extremely impressive. In Somerset there were at one time 6,000 men in arms, in Herefordshire 3,000. The Berkshire Clubmen reckoned they could count on 16,000 followers, and the Clubmen of Wiltshire and Dorset claimed to be able to raise 20,000 men at forty-eight hours' notice. Here is the conservative version of popular action, with the common people desperate to return to 'ancient ways', and not at all eager for a new society.

The character of the Clubmen movements may serve as a token of the new perspective into which many recent historians have put radicalism in the English Revolution. It must be conceded that radical action had a limited impact on events, and that the cause of the radicals and the cause of the people were not always seen as one. Yet the importance of radical ideas to the political and religious ferment of these years cannot be ignored. The world was not turned upside down in mid-seventeenth-century England: but many men hoped, and even more feared, that it might be. This was the contribution of the radicals.

References

Allen, J.W. 1938: *English Political Thought 1603–1660*, vol. I, 1603–1644. London.

Aylmer, G.E. 1968: 'England's spirit unfoulded'. *Past and Present*, 40, 3–15.

Aylmer, G.E. 1970: 'Gentlemen Levellers?'. *Past and Present*, 49, 120–5.

Aylmer, G.E. 1975: *The Levellers in the English Revolution*. London.

Brailsford, H.N. 1976: *The Levellers and the English Revolution*. Edited by Christopher Hill. London.

Capp, B.S. 1972: *The Fifth Monarchy Men*. London.

Cole, Alan 1956: 'The Quakers and the English Revolution'. *Past and Present*, 10, 39–54.

Cole, Alan 1957: 'The social origins of the Early Friends'. *Journal of the Friends' Historical Society*, 48, 99–118.

Collinson, Patrick 1982: *The Religion of Protestants*. Oxford.

Cross, Claire 1972: 'The church of England 1646–1660'. In G.E. Aylmer (ed.), *The Interregnum: The Quest for Settlement 1646–1660*, London.

Erskine-Hill, Howard and Storey, Graham (eds) 1983: *Revolutionary Prose of the English Civil War*. Cambridge.

Everitt, Alan 1966: *The Community of Kent and the Great Rebellion*. Leicester.

Fink, Z.S. 1945: *The Classical Republicans*. Evanston, Illinois.

Fletcher, Anthony 1975: *A County Community in Peace and War: Sussex 1600–1660*. London.

Fletcher, Anthony 1981: *The Outbreak of the English Civil War*. London.

Frank, Joseph 1955: *The Levellers*. New York.

Greaves, Richard L. and Zaller, Robert (eds) 1982: *Biographical Dictionary of British Radicals in the Seventeenth Century*, vol. I: A–F. Brighton.

Greaves, Richard L. and Zaller, Robert (eds) 1983: *Biographical Dictionary of British Radicals in the Seventeenth Century*, vol. II: G–O. Brighton.

Greaves, Richard L. and Zaller, Robert (eds) 1984: *Biographical Dictionary of British Radicals in the Seventeenth Century*, vol. III: P–Z. Brighton.

Gregg, Pauline 1961: *Free-born John*. London.

Haller, William (ed.) 1933–4: *Tracts on Liberty in the Puritan Revolution* (3 vols). New York.

Haller, William and Davies, Godfrey (eds) 1944: *The Leveller Tracts 1647–1653*. New York.

Heinemann, Margot 1978: 'Popular drama and Leveller style – Richard Overton and John Harris'. In Maurice Cornforth (ed.), *Rebels and their Causes*, London.

Hill, Christopher 1958: 'The Norman Yoke'. In his *Puritanism and Revolution*, London.

Hill, Christopher 1971: *Anti-Christ in Seventeenth-Century England*. London.

Hill, Christopher (ed.) 1973: *Winstanley: The Law of Freedom and other Writings*. London.

Hill, Christopher 1974: *Change and Continuity in Seventeenth-Century England*. London.

Hill, Christopher 1975: *The World Turned Upside Down* (Penguin edn). London.

Hill, Christopher 1977: *Milton and the English Revolution*. London.

Hill, Christopher 1978a: 'From Lollards to Levellers'. In Maurice Cornforth (ed.), *Rebels and their Causes*, London.

Hill, Christopher 1978b: 'The religion of Gerrard Winstanley'. *Past and Present*, supplement 5.

Hill, Christopher 1981: 'Parliament and people in seventeenth-century England'. *Past and Present*, 92, 100–24.

Hill, Christopher 1984: *The Experience of Defeat*. London.

Hill, Christopher, Reay, Barry and Lamont, William 1983: *The World of the Muggletonians*. London.

Hirst, Derek 1975: *The Representative of the People?* Cambridge.

Judson, Margaret Atwood 1949: *The Crisis of the Constitution*. New Brunswick.

Kenyon, J.P. (ed.) 1966: *The Stuart Constitution*. Cambridge.

Kishlansky, Mark 1978: 'The case of the army truly stated: The creation of the New Model Army'. *Past and Present*, 81, 51–75.

Kishlansky, Mark 1979a: 'The army and the Levellers: The roads to Putney'. *Historical Journal*, 22, 795–824.

Kishlansky, Mark 1979b: *The Rise of the New Model Army*. Cambridge.

Knachel, Philip A. (ed.) 1969: *The Case of the Commonwealth of England, Stated. By Marchamont Nedham*. Charlottesville.

Lamont, William M. 1969: *Godly Rule*. London.

Lindley, Keith 1982: *Fenland Riots and the English Revolution*. London.

Macpherson, C.B. 1964: *The Political Theory of Possessive Individualism* (paperback edn). Oxford.

Macpherson, C.B. (ed.) 1968: *Hobbes: Leviathan*. London.

Manning, Brian 1976: *The English People and the English Revolution*. London.

Manning, Brian 1978: 'Puritanism and democracy, 1640–1642'. In Donald Pennington and Keith Thomas (eds), *Puritans and Revolutionaries*, Oxford.

Morrill, J.S. 1974: *Cheshire, 1630–1660*. Oxford.

Morrill, J.S. 1976: *The Revolt of the Provinces*. London.

Morrill, John 1982: 'The church in England, 1642–9'. In John Morrill (ed.), *Reactions to the English Civil War 1642–1649*, London.

Morton, A.L. 1970: *The World of the Ranters*. London.

Morton, A.L. 1975: *Freedom in Arms: A Selection of Leveller Writings*. London.

Nuttall, Geoffrey 1946: *The Holy Spirit in Puritan Faith and Experience*. Oxford.

Petegorsky, David W. 1940: *Left-Wing Democracy in the English Civil War*. London.

Pocock, J.G.A. 1957: *The Ancient Constitution and the Feudal Law*. Cambridge.

Pocock, J.G.A. (ed.) 1977: *The Political Works of James Harrington*. Cambridge.

Rabb, Theodore K. 1981: 'The role of the Commons'. *Past and Present*, 92, 55–78.

Reay, Barry 1980a: 'Quaker opposition to tithes 1652–1660'. *Past and Present*, 86, 98–120.

Reay, Barry 1980b: 'The social origins of early Quakerism'. *Journal of Interdisciplinary History*, 11, 55–72.

Russell, Conrad 1976: 'Parliamentary history in perspective 1604–1629'. *History*, 61, 1–27.

Russell, Conrad 1979: *Parliaments and English Politics 1621–1629*. Oxford.

Russell, Conrad 1983: 'The nature of a parliament in early Stuart England'. In Howard Tomlinson (ed.), *Before the English Civil War*, London.

Sabine, G.H. (ed.) 1941: *The Works of Gerrard Winstanley*. New York.

Schenk, W. 1948: *The Concern for Social Justice in the Puritan Revolution*. London.

Schochet, Gordon J. 1975: *Patriarchalism and Political Thought*. Oxford.

Sharp, Andrew (ed.) 1983: *Political ideas of the English Civil Wars 1641–1649*. London.

Sharp, Buchanan 1980: *In Contempt of All Authority*. Berkeley, California.

Sharpe, Kevin 1983: 'The Personal Rule of Charles I'. In Howard Tomlinson (ed.), *Before the English Civil War*, London.

Shaw, Howard 1968: *The Levellers*. London.

Skinner, Quentin 1972: 'Conquest and consent: Thomas Hobbes and the engagement controversy'. In G.E. Aylmer (ed.), *The Interregnum: The Quest for Settlement 1646–1660*, London.

Smith, Nigel 1983: *A Collection of Ranter Writings from the 17th Century*. London.

Thomas, David 1983: 'Financial and administrative developments'. In Howard Tomlinson (ed.), *Before the English Civil War*, London.

Thomas, Keith 1958: 'Women and the Civil War sects'. *Past and Present*, 13, 42–57.

Thomas, Keith 1965: 'The social origins of Hobbes's political thought'. In K.C. Brown (ed.), *Hobbes Studies*, Oxford.

Thomas, Keith 1969: 'Another Digger broadside'. *Past and Present*, 42, 57–68.

Thomas, Keith 1972: 'The Levellers and the franchise'. In G.E. Aylmer (ed.), *The Interregnum: The Quest for Settlement 1646–1660*, London.

Thompson, Christopher 1980: 'Maximilian Petty and the Putney debate on the franchise'. *Past and Present*, 88, 63–9.

Tolmie, Murray 1977: *The Triumph of the Saints*. Cambridge.

Tuck, Richard 1979: *Natural Rights Theories*. Cambridge.

Tyacke, Nicholas 1973: 'Puritanism, Arminianism and counter-revolution'. In Conrad Russell (ed.), *The Origins of the English Civil War*, London.

Underdown, David 1973: *Somerset in the Civil War and Interregnum*. Newton Abbott.

Underdown, David 1978: ' "Honest" radicals in the counties, 1642–1649'. In Donald Pennington and Keith Thomas (eds), *Puritans and Revolutionaries*, Oxford.

Underdown, David 1979: 'The chalk and the cheese: Contrasts among the English Clubmen'. Past and Present, 85, 25–48.

Underdown, David 1980: 'Community and class: Theories of local politics in the English Revolution'. In B.C. Malament (ed.), *After the Reformation*, Manchester.

Vann, R.T. 1969: 'Quakerism and the social structure in the Interregnum'. *Past and Present*, 43, 71–91.

Walter, John 1980: 'Grain riots and popular attitudes to the law'. In John Brewer and John Styles (eds), *An Ungovernable People*, London.

Walter, John and Wrightson, Keith 1976: 'Dearth and the social order in early modern England'. *Past and Present*, 71, 22–42.

Walzer, Michael 1964: 'Puritanism as a revolutionary ideology'. *History and Theory*, 3, 59–90.

Walzer, Michael 1965: *The Revolution of the Saints*. Cambridge, Massachusetts.

Weston, C.C. 1960: 'The theory of mixed monarchy under Charles I and after'. *English Historical Review*, 75, 426–43.

White, B.R. 1966: 'The organisation of the Particular Baptists, 1644–1660'. *Journal of Ecclesiastical History*, 17, 109–226.

Wolfe, Don M. (ed.) 1944: *Leveller Manifestoes of the Puritan Revolution*. New York.

Woodhouse, A.S.P. 1974: *Puritanism and Liberty* (2nd edn with a preface by Ivan Roots). London.

Woolrych, Austin (ed.) 1974: *Complete Prose Works of John Milton*. vol. VII, 1659–1660. New Haven and London.

Woolrych, Austin 1980: 'Political theory and political practice'. In C.A. Patrides and Raymond B. Waddington (eds), *The Age of Milton*, Manchester.

Woolrych, Austin 1982: *Commonwealth to Protectorate*. Oxford.

Worden, Blair 1974: *The Rump Parliament*. Cambridge.

Worden, Blair 1981: 'Classical republicanism and the Puritan revolution'. In Hugh Lloyd-Jones, Valerie Pearl and Blair Worden (eds), *History and Imagination*, London.

Zagorin, Perez 1954: *A History of Political Thought in the English Revolution*. London.

Index